# Gardens of the South

Southern Accents Press

# *Gardens of the South*

Simon and Schuster
New York

FRONTISPIECE

The entrance to Biltmore Estate Gardens in Asheville, North Carolina.


OPPOSITE INTRODUCTION

The formal English Walled Garden at Biltmore Estate.


This book consists of revised and enlarged essays originally published in SOUTHERN ACCENTS magazine.

Copyright© 1985 by W.R.C. Smith Publishing Company.
All rights reserved including the right of reproduction in whole or in part in any form.
SOUTHERN ACCENTS is a registered trademark of W.R.C. Smith Publishing Company in the United States Trademark Office.
Southern Accents Press is a division of W.R.C. Smith Publishing Company
1760 Peachtree Road, N.W., Atlanta, Georgia 30357

Published by Simon and Schuster, a Division of Simon & Schuster, Inc., Simon & Schuster Building, Rockefeller Center
1230 Avenue of the Americas, New York, New York 10020

SIMON AND SCHUSTER and colophon are registered trademarks of Simon & Schuster, Inc.

Manufactured in Italy


First Printing 1985
1 2 3 4 5 6 7 8 9 10
Library of Congress Cataloging in Publication Data
ISBN: 0-671-60191-1

# Contents

# Introduction

Probably the greatest reward of gardening in the South is character development. The Southern gardener, if he survives, will acquire patience, humility, stoicism, and irrepressible optimism in the face of devastating odds. The climate in Dixie is notoriously capricious, and in recent years almost every month has been a record-breaker — the coldest January, the wettest April, and the hottest and driest August.

The gardening season seems endless, with chrysanthemums still blooming in November and daffodils popping up in February, and in the brief midwinter respite, the gardener must cope with garden plans and seed catalogs. The fact is, the Southern horticulturist faces a twelve-month grind involving an enormous expenditure of time and money. It sometimes seems that greenbacks are more essential to a flourishing garden than green thumbs. Certainly there are times when even the most ardent gardener envies Adam and Eve for being expelled from Eden.

And yet there will come the rare day when — in my own garden, for example — the jet of a fountain glitters in the spring sun, when the elusive scent of boxwood mingles with the fragrance of pale shaggy peonies, when hosts of early daisies cluster about the spires of foxgloves and a multitude of rosebuds flutters in the breeze. Then all the months of travail are forgotten; for a euphoric moment the gardener has the sense of having tamed Nature; even of having taught her a few tricks.

Improving on Nature is, after all, what gardening is about. When the French rococo painter François Boucher was criticized for the artificiality of his landscapes, he replied that in fact Nature was too green and badly lit. Like Boucher, the gardener employs artifice to create a more ideal setting than Nature will ever devise. When visiting the various gardens in this book — whether strolling the meandering paths shaded by live oaks and cypresses at Magnolia or marveling at the formal beauty of Bayou Bend's clipped hedges, statues and fountains — one recognizes the authority of the design. In the best gardens nothing is haphazard or arbitrary, and however artfully the plan is concealed, however ''naturalistic'' the effect, nothing is really natural. Like the artist, the gardener imposes order on chaos.

Instead of using oil colors or pastels, the gardener paints with plants. While the Southern gardener has a profusion of native and exotic plant material from which to choose, his selection is limited by the exigencies of climate and the dictates of style. Delicate flowers like delphinium, primrose and columbine wither in the relentless heat of Southern summers; and if, as it now seems, winters in the South are becoming increasingly severe, the camellia, gardenia and Indian azalea may have to be confined to the greenhouse. And due to the vagaries of fashion, such cheerful plants as cannas, larkspurs, dahlias and geraniums have been banished from many elegant gardens, for the gardening snob shares with the social snob an abhorrence of everything that is commonplace.

Whether snobbish or populist, every garden is different; and the variety in this volume is impressive, ranging geographically from Delaware south to Florida and west to Texas. There are the vast public gardens like Winterthur, Biltmore and Bellingrath whose scope dumbfounds us, and the minuscule private ones like Mrs. Henry Tompkins' and the Homer Deakinses which beguile us with their precision. The oldest is Middleton Place, created in the 1740's, while the Tench Coxes in their small cloistered garden have achieved a mature look in a mere dozen years.

The fortunate reader of *Gardens of the South* can hobnob with the shades of colonial governors at Tryon Palace or with those of presidents at the White House; he can admire the horticultural triumphs of seasoned gardeners like Jim Gibbs, Ryan Gainey and Mrs. Thomas Martin, luxuriate in the provincial charm at Frances and DeJongh Franklins', or drift on the lagoons at Cypress. He can, in a word, enjoy all these splendors by merely turning these pages, without shedding the sweat and tears that have watered every garden since Eden.

*William Nathaniel Banks*

*William Nathaniel Banks*

# Private Gardens

# Villa Caro

In 1400, during the time of the Italian Renaissance, architects visualized gardens as transitional zones between buildings and the surrounding countryside. With this in mind, they designed planting spaces as extensions of their houses. In many ways, architect Albert Howell paid homage to this past when he designed his own house and the surrounding gardens. His design achieves a balance between simplicity and sophistication in a setting that, although formal, never seems contrived.

The site is deceiving. At first glance it appears to be gentle and rolling, but in reality, the back drops sharply into a ravine before it ascends straight up a rugged hillside, a topographical irregularity the planner used as an asset. Tall, leafy trees and shrubs that stretch across the front of the property obscure the house from the road and provide both privacy and proper spatial definition. In the midst of this natural architecture stands the house, its pastel walls and tile roof representative of the style of southern Italian villas.

A cobblestone walkway leading through a sweep of green lawn emphasizes the facade. Two heroic stone statues grace each corner of a semi-circular garden which is outlined on the perimeter by towering ligustrum that is reiterated along the inner edge with boxwood and, in summer, a stand of variegated hosta lilies. Such lush areas were greatly admired by the ancients. Considered a luxury because of their demand for water, they were usually planted near the house so that the green could be constantly admired.

Each summer this classical landscape surrenders to an extravagant display of hydrangeas that bloom in great profusion around the house. Their huge pink and blue blossoms flowering against warm pink stucco walls present quite a spectacle.

The hydrangea, a beautiful and bountiful shrub, takes its name from the Greek — *hydor*, meaning water, and *aggeion*, meaning vase, the latter descriptive of its cup-shaped blossom. Blooms range in color from white through pink to violet depending somewhat on the pH and aluminum content of the soil. They require moist, leafy soil and will not tolerate hot sun or drought.

Hydrangeas were introduced to this garden in the 1920's by a wily Scotsman, William Hunter, who advised the owners to avoid "fancy" plants and stick instead to natural varieties. Following this advice, they learned to propagate the plant from summer cuttings which has resulted in this wealth of blooming plants. Such gardening practices faithfully adhere to the earlier precepts of Henry du Pont, owner and creator of the Winterthur gardens in Delaware, who advised planting boldly in large masses, making use of indigenous trees and working out a color scheme with care.

The side garden is also planted with hydrangeas and features an unusual curved stone bench as its focal point. The vista from the rear colonnaded promenade is across an open section of lawn to a balustrade adorned with stone obelisks, fruit baskets and statues of cherubs.

In his essay "Of Gardens," Francis Bacon wrote, "God Almighty first planted a Garden. And indeed it is the purest of Human pleasures. It is the Greatest refreshment to the Spirits of Man; without which Buildings and Pallaces are but Grosse Handy-Works . . ."

LEFT: *Boxwoods and dogwoods form a soft background for a curved stone bench secured at each side by seasonal garden statues. Hydrangeas bloom on either side of a tapis vert.*

ABOVE: *Hydrangeas in tones of blue and pink are the major theme throughout the villa grounds. Cobblestone walkways lead to a semicircular garden where a tall hedge of ligustrum defines the outer edge followed by boxwoods and in summer, hosta lilies.*

FOLLOWING PAGES: *Throughout the long summer, pink and blue hydrangeas blooming against pink stucco walls create a jewel-like setting for the small, perfect Italianate villa.*

ABOVE: *An array of garden statues graces the stone balustrade framing the back lawn. In summer, beds are planted with shade-loving plants such as impatiens, ferns, begonias and peonies.*

FACING PAGE: *Light diffused by swaying weeping willows casts a soft glow through the arches of the villa to the Italian tile entranceway.*

# Country Cottage

The most glorious of all flower displays appears in the nostalgic and romantic cottage-style garden. Regardless of size, such spaces are distinguished by beds filled with an infinite variety of plants that bloom in masses of riotous color. Designed as living tapestries, the colors and textures of these gardens intermingle in patterns that are constantly changing.

Professional planter and designer Ryan Gainey specializes in old-time Southern gardens. His approach is much the same as that of an artist beginning a landscape painting. Using the ground as his canvas and the flowers as his palette, he weaves a pattern using different shapes, colors and textures of plants in his design.

Gainey's fascination with gardening is rooted in nostalgic memories of his great-grandmother's garden in the country where flowers grew in long, full rows. The fragrance of such flowers as nicotiana, roses, gardenias and geraniums created an early and lasting impression that led to a college major in horticulture and a degree that later blossomed into a thriving business.

Recently his sensitivities reached new heights while he was visiting Giverny, the paradisiacal refuge of painter Claude Monet near Vernon, France. Here he gratified his senses and absorbed the ideas of the Impressionist who planted flower gardens that were as masterly as his canvases. Upon his return, Gainey determined to put his accumulation of memories together in his own garden. Choosing a site that had been an early 20th-century nursery, he began to cultivate and experiment with old-fashioned varieties that had been missing from plant lists for years. Traveling through the South with trowel in hand, he dug bulbs and bushes from roadside banks and begged seeds, cuttings and flowers until his garden abounded in long-forgotten species. His expertise in reestablishing these old varieties put him on the leading edge of a resurgence of interest in country-cottage gardens that is sweeping the land.

Gainey's own garden, filled to overflowing with unusual plants and shrubs, is entered through an arbor draped by an ancient mimosa or silk tree. Stone urns planted with hardy 'New Guinea' impatiens anchor a crisp white picket fence that stretches around the house and garden. The fence provides a unifying element that suggests enclosure without blocking the brightly colored flowers. Forgotten examples of evening primroses, larkspurs, coreopsis, yellow violets, peonies and poppies present a mille fleurs tapestry of color.

Behind the house is a double border where flowers growing in rows renew Gainey's childhood memories and offer an ever-changing vista of seasonal color and texture. In spring, iris, standard azaleas and pansies burst upon the scene. Annual vines scramble over stick arbors in summer and foxgloves, delphiniums, Canterbury bells, astilbes and veronica overflow their borders into the path. Lobelia, belamcanda and rudeckia end this season as hostas, ligularia and anemones begin. Asters and chrysanthemums create a blaze of autumn color before the garden takes its winter rest.

In this painterly setting where practicality coincides with nostalgia, there is a longing to surrender to sentimentality and indulge in memories of long ago, recorded on canvases and in the artistry of gardeners with vision.

PRECEDING PAGES: *A simple white picket fence and arbor, shaded by a mimosa tree, are an appropriate introduction to this Southern cottage-style garden where familiar varieties of fragrant and colorful flowers bloom from early spring until the first frost.*

ABOVE: *In a shady corner of the garden, a charming stone figure stands amidst a display of hardy impatiens. Ferns and rhododendrons make a placid background for the blossoms of hot pink impatiens.*

RIGHT: *A mass of familiar plants such as Queen Anne's lace, brown-eyed Susans, sweet peas and irises was transplanted from abandoned plots and roadsides into this cottage border.*

ABOVE: *A dry wall of old Tennessee fieldstones is the ideal setting for rockery plants. The tiny ornamental basin tucked into a shady nook affords a welcome retreat for wild creatures.*

RIGHT: *White phlox and Easter lilies create a cooling effect in the border during long, hot days.*

ABOVE: *Terra-cotta containers holding flirtatious purple and lavender 'Streptocarpus' are attached to a weathered gray fence in this country cottage garden.*

FACING PAGE: *In the garden's double border, irises and standard azaleas flower in spring, honeysuckle vines cover the stick arbor in summer, as a riot of perennials and annuals crowds the beds followed by asters and chrysanthemums that end the season in a blaze of autumn color.*

# Brigadoon

The charming town of Highlands, North Carolina, is located in a storybook setting on a high plateau of the Blue Ridge Mountains in the southwestern part of the state, just above the common boundary with South Carolina and Georgia. The tiny municipality of slightly more than 1,000 permanent residents sits astride the Blue Ridge Divide and has long been a mecca for "flatlanders" seeking relief from the heat of summer.

The air is cool and clear and sweet in Highlands: it's the highest (at 4,000 feet) incorporated municipality east of the Mississippi River. And the natural beauty of the area is unsurpassed anywhere in the entire country. Flowering dogwoods, rhododendrons and flame azaleas set the surrounding southern Blue Ridge Mountains ablaze with color.

Just on the outskirts of the little town, on the misty banks of a lake that is part of the Highlands Country Club, is the picturesque home of Mr. and Mrs. D.E. Hughes. Located on a three-and-a-half-acre site overlooking the 18th green, their mountain retreat, called "Brigadoon" after the mythical Scottish town of that name, has become a showplace of the area.

When the Hugheses bought the property, friends despaired that Mrs. Hughes, who does not play golf, tennis or bridge, might be bored. But this energetic lady took up gardening as her recreation, spending hours observing, working, experimenting and learning about local flora from Sadie Talley, a woman who has spent her lifetime caring for flowers in the region.

Because the approach to the house is shady, rhododendron underplanted with hosta and fern mark the entrance; but the sunny side is the setting for Brigadoon's crowning glory. From the house a vista of green grass fans out to the lake and across to the golf course. A rock retaining wall follows the natural curve of the water and serves as the border for a jewel-like English garden. According to Mrs. Hughes, "every flower that the seed catalogs advise will survive in Zone 7" is planted here and as a dividend for passersby the garden is reflected in the surface of the lake's clear water.

Each spring 5,000 daffodils and 85 varieties of iris, along with tulips and crocus are on display within a basic evergreen boxwood design to exhibit a riot of color. In summer perennials such as hollyhocks, foxgloves, larkspurs, delphiniums and phlox return and are joined by annuals and bi-annuals planted in triangular drifts. Bright red geraniums in tubs mark the entrance to the pristine pavilion, called "Swan Inn" where, to complete the idyllic setting, a family of swans obligingly swims in the placid lake.

A gentle hill overlooking the pavilion is perhaps the best spot of all at Brigadoon: a quiet, marvelously tended area with a magnificent fountain. Pink and white dogwoods dot the pathway to it, and all about is a profusion of color. Nearby, 50 varieties of lilies flourish, and white Shasta daisies abound. The gardens, kept in immaculate condition by Mrs. Hughes, are divided into an English cutting garden and separate gardens for dahlias, ferns and peonies.

Brigadoon is just as magical and inviting as Highlands itself, and the home, the pavilion and the gardens bespeak the gentility of its owners, past and present.

FACING PAGE: *Swan Inn overlooks the lake and the 18th green of the golf course beyond. An English country garden filled with an endless variety of plants borders a flagstone patio. Flowers blooming continuously throughout the summer bring admiring comments from passersby.*

ABOVE: *This exquisite example of hybrid lily is lilac-pink and crimson-spotted with outward-facing flowers and curved petals. With approximately 16 flowers per stem, it grows to a height of 3¼ feet and blooms in July.*

ABOVE: *Brigadoon's lake-side setting in Highlands, North Carolina, evokes images of Scotland for its owners, Mr. and Mrs. D.E. Hughes. White daisies blooming along a rock retaining wall border a garden that rises up the hillside in a sunburst of color that changes with the seasons.*

RIGHT: *White 'Alaska' daisies are reflected in the clear water where ducks and swans, swimming in graceful patterns, enjoy the lake.*

FACING PAGE: *Brilliant red geraniums planted every 14 feet along the waters' edge provide color in the midst of a border of white daisies.*

# French Flavor

A cobbled courtyard, stucco walls rising to high gables, a gnarled wisteria vine trained to cloak the front door in the shape of a leafy-green porte cochere, with a creek that meanders quietly by all, could easily be a scene set in the French countryside near Burgundy. But such is not the case, for this beautifully crafted residence, bounded by colorful arbors and intimate walled gardens is situated in a conventional neighborhood in the heart of a busy Southern city.

Still, the flavor of France is all-pervasive. The first of several garden vignettes is a formal parterre design with four distinctive squares outlined by pea gravel pathways. Each square is edged with juniper and holds a topiary rose in the center surrounded by four miniature roses. Two of the topiaries are 'First Prize' and two are 'Royal Highness.' The miniature roses are 'Rosmarin' and 'Chipper.' White and pink flowers have been added to the beds in honor of a forthcoming garden wedding. Included are English daisies, foxgloves, begonias, delphiniums, 'New Guinea' impatiens and Queen Anne's lace chosen to complement the romantic occasion.

The parterre style is characterized by surface patterns and endures as one of the oldest and most often used garden designs. Beds are frequently outlined with brick or stone since these materials are more suitable for this purpose than plants. Parterres can be large or small, and the range of plant material within the beds is left entirely to the desires of the gardener.

Another of the vignettes is a secluded, secret garden where clipped ilex surrounds the base of

*Camellia sasanquas* espaliered against weathered stucco walls. Two lattice panels covered in euonymus frame an unusual lead ram's-head fountain and form a soft background for an enchantingly pretty cottage-style border. This type of border is designed to have some plants beginning to bloom as others start to fade. They are often planted with shrubs, perennials or a combination of both, making them a perfect foundation. In this garden, the bed is composed of perennials such as leopard's-bane, aquilegia, Regale lily, veronica, centaurea and foxglove along with others that bloom in early spring and those that last until the first frost.

An ilex hedge separates the secret garden from a plantation of hybrid tea roses in a wide range of colors and varieties. These include 'Mr. Lincoln' and 'Chrysler Imperial' in red; 'Honor' and 'Pristine' in white; 'Oregold,' apricot, 'Savannah' and 'Georgia' in gold; 'Louisiana' and 'Garden Party' in cream; 'Sweet Surrender,' 'Electron,' 'Radiance,' and 'Queen Elizabeth' in pink.

A rail fence with an old wood and cast iron gate from France makes an inviting entrance into the informal part of the garden. Here, color continues to play a leading role. Against a natural woodland backdrop that leads down a hillside to the creek, plantings of 'Annabelle' hydrangeas, azaleas, impatiens, 'Anna Rose Whitney' rhododendrons, dogwoods and begonias along with a mixed bed of floribunda, grandiflora and hybrid tea roses create a breathtaking display of tone and texture.

At the heart of the design is a brick terrace shaded by a very old scuppernong vine. Here family and friends gather to enjoy the pleasant sights, sounds and scents of this charming garden.

FACING PAGE: *Masses of blooming begonias establish the border for beds of roses in the back garden. An old window, imaginatively recycled from a house in France, makes a charming gate.*

ABOVE: *Gravel and brick paths lead between beds of multi-colored roses in this section of walled garden. Beyond the wood fence is an old-fashioned perennial border.*

FOLLOWING PAGES: *Brick-edged pea gravel walkways divide beds in the parterre garden. Juniper-edged squares in the formal section hold a topiary rose surrounded by miniature roses, while in the cutting area, numerous varieties of roses are cultivated behind clipped ilex-edged beds.*

29

ABOVE: *Euonymus-covered lattice panels on either side of a ram's head fountain create a pleasing background for perennials such as leopard's-bane, aquilegia, Regale lily and foxglove that bloom throughout the summer months.*

FACING PAGE: *Planters holding weeping cherry trees stand on either side of the arched entryway, cloaked in a wisteria canopy. A vintage street lantern from Holland contributes to the charm of the Country French-style house.*

# Topiary Magic

Harvey S. Ladew was the kind of man about whom novels are written. An adventurer, a romantic and a gentleman of boundless energy, he had it all: good looks, style, wealth and good humor. At the entrance to his rose garden, on a flight of steps, is a Chinese proverb: "To be happy for a week take a wife; to be happy for a month kill your pig and eat it; but to be happy all your life be a gardener." If this be true, there is no doubt that Harvey S. Ladew was happy all his life.

Ladew's zest for living combined with a passion for fox hunting inspired his move from Long Island, New York, to the Maryland hunt country. He bought Pleasant Valley Farm near Monkton in 1929 and set about transforming the tranquil countryside into a garden extravaganza.

The idea for this fantasy landscape sprang from a topiary of a huntsman riding to hounds he chanced to spy while on a visit to England. Intrigued by this art of trimming trees, hedges and shrubs into ornamental shapes, he decided to create a topiary garden on his own 250-acre estate. With great gusto and imagination he decided to do all the landscape planning himself. One project led to another, and before his death in 1976, at age 89, he had created 20 different "theme" gardens, all interspersed with topiary.

From the entrance to the estate, the driveway passes a gardener's cottage and then the first whimsy: a topiary fox-hunting scene clipped out of Japanese yew. The driveway leads past the main house, where a Wildflower Garden is set among tall shade trees underplanted with rhododendrons, wild phlox, bloodroot and violets.

A path leads through a tunnel of rhododendrons to a Victorian Garden. Flowers here are mostly in shades of blue and lavender, with a three-tiered cast-iron fountain serving as a focal point. Exiting through a topiary archway, the passageway is planted on both sides with shrubs that display brilliant berries in autumn. Steps descend to a croquet court where crescent beds are massed with pink and blue flowers, roses, phlox and Siberian irises.

Next is the Pink Garden, where an assortment of ornamental cherries, crab apples, dogwoods, azaleas, fairy roses, astilbes, weigela and rhododendrons is featured.

But the most fascinating of all the wonders at Ladew are three vast terraces with hemlock hedges sculptured into obelisks, garlands, windows and hens sitting on nests. A flight of brick steps leads downhill to an oval fountain in the middle of the Great Bowl, then up beyond to an avenue of massive topiary hedges along a vista to a distant hill crowned with a Temple of Venus. A yew hedge bordering the Iris Garden is trimmed to simulate swans gliding along gentle waves, and in the Iris Garden a Chinese junk complete with sails, a massive Buddha and a giraffe, all in clipped evergreens, continue the topiary theme.

One of Harvey Ladew's most outstanding achievements was a Distinguished Service Medal awarded five years before his death from the Garden Club of America in recognition of his "great interest in developing and maintaining the most outstanding topiary garden in America without professional help."

FACING PAGE: *A massive topiary hedge lines the grassy avenue to a distant hill which is crowned with a Temple of Venus.*

ABOVE: *Three vast terraces exhibit meticulously tended box and cone figures bordered by intricate garlanded topiary walls. In the background is Pleasant Valley House, an old clapboard farmhouse reminiscent of a Southern plantation, remodeled by Ladew as his Maryland home.*

LEFT: *A close-up of whimsical but intrepid topiary huntsman frozen forever in time.*

FOLLOWING PAGES: *Cartoon-like topiary figures clipped from Japanese yew depict a horse and rider jumping a gate while riding to hounds.*

FACING PAGE: *Lovely Siberian irises border a stream in one of the many theme gardens planted amidst the sculptured forms of Ladew Topiary Gardens.*

ABOVE: *In spring, the Yellow Garden is alive with flowers and shrubs as bright as sunshine. Japanese maples and flame azaleas contribute to the Oriental flavor of this brilliant setting.*

# Romantic Cloister

No one would even guess it's there. Hidden behind a stucco wall on a quiet street, this garden is not for public show, but rather for the pleasure of the owners and their guests. It is an extension of their house, walled in and secluded.

The design draws heavily on history: the concept of a walled garden integrated with a house isn't new. The Mesopotamians put up reed and thorn fences around gardens near their homes and raised fruit, vegetables and medicinal herbs within the protective confines. In Egypt, men of wealth developed gardens for pleasure, enclosing formal, rectilinear spaces adjacent to their houses with high brick walls broken in places by decorative gateways. The Greeks are credited with adding pools to the center of their gardens, a concept later adopted by the Romans.

Walled gardens in Western Europe were first built by religious orders. Within cloisters, herbs and flowers were raised for altar and shrine decorations. The French eventually broke with the walled concept, creating immense parks for the delight of the rich and royal. During the late 16th and early 17th centuries, the classic French garden, with its sense of order, logic and discipline, was adapted from earlier Roman layouts by the eminent garden artist André Le Nôtre. His belief that a garden could express a spirit of logical order, in the same way as painting, architecture or music, influenced all of Europe.

The English, drawing from this formal French style, developed the first true landscape gardening. Their huge "picture gardens," designed by Henry Hoare and later Lancelot "Capability" Brown, were on a grand scale and included lakes, bridges and sweeping lawns.

But time has run full circle, and now the trend is toward a return to the earlier concept in which house and walled gardens form a living unit. The plan for the garden here was conceived by noted architect James Means at the time he designed the house, and combines French, English and Chinese influences with a bit of Georgia history for flavor. It was inspired by a section of the classical formal gardens at the Château de Villandry, considered one of the most beautiful in France. Within this carefully structured plan, the owners have created an informal romanticism in the English manner, placing great value on the character and beauty of individual plants.

The gazebo is reminiscent of the Chinese pagoda, a style popular in both French and English gardens of the 16th century, and is built of beams from a 100-year-old house in Elberton, Georgia. This architectural element offers a sheltered retreat for entertaining or quiet contemplation. Walkways of crab orchard stone edged with brick lead between flower beds. These are filled with such old-fashioned plants as coral bells, baptisia and princess roses, all of which were transplanted from a family garden in Biltmore Forest, North Carolina, and are difficult to find in nurseries today. Other plants include Queen Elizabeth roses, irises, lilies, peonies, pinks, candytuft, climbing Peace roses, daisies, Concord grapes and white wisteria.

As people have known throughout the ages, a garden is not just a showplace for plants. It is an extension of the home as well, meant to exist as a living space for people.

LEFT: *Crab orchard stone pathways edged in brick, distinguish beds in this parterre garden abloom with roses, peonies, irises, coral bells and baptisia. The center is planted with primroses; a container holds a mock orange, Philadelphus, which bears fruit.*

ABOVE: *A graceful terra-cotta swan planted with pink geraniums surveys the scene from a perch inside the garden gazebo.*

FOLLOWING PAGES: *Designed as a place to relax and entertain, the gazebo, built of weathered beams from an old house, complements the old-fashioned flowers in the garden. Fragrant roses, espaliered against the side of the house, bloom profusely throughout the summer.*

# The White House

The White House gardens in Washington, D.C., where the nation's First Family entertains visitors from all over the world, have a checkered history. Although a number of presidents and First Ladies contributed to their development, it has been only in recent years that the beautifully manicured gardens have been transformed into a proper adjunct to the Executive Mansion.

George Washington chose the site for the executive residence, and in 1792 Irish architect James Hoban won a competition to design the mansion and grounds. In colonial days it was the vogue for a house to stand clear on its understructure with no close landscaping. Most often there were ornamental trees and a seasonal flower bed in front and a more formal garden located behind the house.

John Quincy Adams loved growing things. He had a spring-and-summer garden at the White House, and his diary described his plantings as "a small garden of less than two acres," yet it contained a variety of flora: "forest and fruit trees, shrubs, hedges, esculent vegetables, kitchen and medicinal herbs, hot house plants, flowers and weeds, to the amount, I conjecture, of at least one thousand."

In 1913, Mrs. Woodrow Wilson made an attempt to create a garden retreat for the President by planting roses in an area adjoining the executive office. No significant changes were made in Mrs. Wilson's rose garden until 1961, when President John F. Kennedy returned from an official trip to Europe where he had visited with heads of state in their gardens. Now being aware of the shortcomings of the White House plantings, President Kennedy asked Mrs. Paul Mellon to undertake the task of redesigning the Rose Garden and the East Garden adjacent to the East Wing colonnade. White House horticulturalists Irvin Williams and Harold Green helped implement Mrs. Mellon's plans.

Today the Rose Garden is a rectangular plot about fifty feet wide and a hundred feet long. Its central lawn is bordered on the north and south sides by beds planted with low hedges of holly and boxwood, along with various bushes, seasonal flowers and flowering crab apple trees.

The East Garden, which was officially declared the Jacqueline Kennedy Garden in 1965 by Mrs. Lyndon Johnson, is approximately the same size as the Rose Garden. It has a slightly smaller central lawn bordered on both sides by plantings of clipped American hollies, seasonal flowers and herbs used by the White House chef. At one end is a pergola paved with old brick; at the other is a decorative pool. The Rose Garden is mentioned more often in the national news, but both gardens are used frequently for receptions and entertaining by the First Family.

John Quincy Adams would never recognize his backyard garden of "esculent vegetables . . . flowers and weeds" today. It has been replaced by sophisticated and lovely gardens that are fitting parts of our nation's most famous residence.

In earlier years the gardens were open to the public, but it has become necessary to provide greater security and privacy for the President and his guests and, unfortunately, the gardens are now closed to viewers.

FACING PAGE: *Brilliant flowers such as chrysanthemums mixed with white salvia and* Anemone japonica *are planted in the Rose Garden each fall, and because the garden faces south, bloom far into autumn. President Kennedy had flagstone steps constructed so that he could greet distinguished visitors in a garden setting.*

ABOVE: *The East Garden has two rectangular planting beds bordered by dwarf pillow boxwoods. Centering alternate squares in the beds are topiaried American holly trees.*

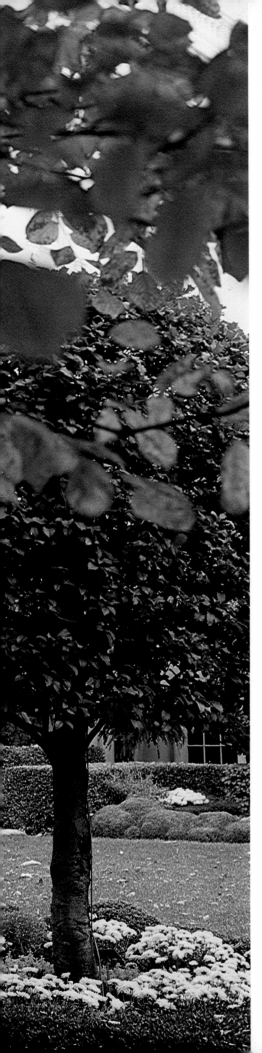

LEFT: *In the East Garden, a white-columned pergola paved with old brick provides a pleasant area where the First Family and visitors often enjoy the fall flowers at informal receptions.*

ABOVE: *At the other end of the East Garden is a small decorative pool and a statue of a girl with a trowel and flowerpot by Sylvia Shaw Judson.*

ABOVE: *From the President's office one can see the Rose Garden and its small flagstone terrace. Its central lawn is bordered on the north and south sides by beds planted with low hedges of holly and boxwood, along with rose bushes, seasonal flowers and Katherine crab apple trees.*

FACING PAGE: *A pathway connecting wings of the White House flanks the East Garden. Topiaried American holly trees accent beds underplanted with seasonal flowers.*

# Formal Cityscape

This small formal garden was planned by noted architect Neel Reid in the mid-1920's and survives as one of the most pleasing examples of his work. Establishing a direct relationship between the house and garden was Reid's hallmark. He envisioned the design of a property as a whole. He felt that no one part should be considered independently and that the architect of the house should also be the architect of the garden.

The library of the home extends into the garden area, which is a flat, rectangular excavation into a hillside that slopes upward from the house. Retaining walls of granite buttress the perimeter on each side and at the rear, where two graceful flights of stone steps ascend to the top of the wall and lead to a guesthouse designed with a classic columned portico. This structure functions as well as an architectural accent in the garden.

The original garden featured a square pool enhanced by a green carpet of grass. On either side of the grass were two box-bordered flower beds with walks between them of old brick laid in sand. The beds featured colorful flowers such as tulips, phlox, iris and narcissus in spring, peonies and larkspur in summer and chrysanthemums in fall. English ivy was trained against the garden walls, and alternating roses, 'Doctor Van Fleet' and 'Silver Moon,' cascaded over the walls. Above the walls were flowering shrubs such as forsythia, January jasmine, spirea, crape myrtle and gardenia. Wisteria, ginger lilies of the valley, white azaleas and white irises bordered the house.

As the years passed, the garden became overgrown; the box hedges around the beds were gone, roses and miscellaneous bulbs had overrun the beds, and the white azaleas at the base of the walls had spread over the walkways. The time had come for renewal, so in 1976 landscape designer Julia O. Martin was called upon to revitalize the once beautiful area.

To gain access to the task, the designer began by drastically cutting back the Indica azaleas and trimming them up as hedges. The English ivy-covered walls became more visible, thus giving the white blossoms of the azaleas a dramatic appearance. Flower beds were completely cleared, the soil reworked and mounded in the center to allow for better drainage.

The outer borders of the beds were then outlined in mondo grass and the center mounds planted with the Gumpo azalea called Beth Bullard. This dwarf azalea, which blooms in late May, has an extraordinarily large coral-colored single blossom. The space between the mondo grass border and the Gumpo azaleas was then planted with *ajuga reptans*, a flat-growing ground cover with bronze leaves. Large urns were placed atop the walls and planted with paler pink Gumpo azaleas, providing a lovely accent to the perimeter. Four impish Italian statues were added to the corners of the pool, which remains as originally designed and is planted with water hyacinths, pink, yellow and blue water lilies.

In the style of the 1920's, the original Neel Reid design was filled with a wealth of blooming plants that required the attention of a watchful gardener. Although maintenance has been simplified in the restoration by changes in plant material, the genius of the architect has been preserved.

ABOVE: *The formal garden on an axis with the library was cut out of a hill and walled with granite. It is one of architect Neel Reid's most pleasing designs. Above the garden, the guesthouse is a carefully planned part of the landscape.*

RIGHT: *Four rectangular beds in the garden are planted with Gumpo azaleas surrounded by bronze-leafed ajuga. In the center of each of the azalea areas, pale pink double peonies appear in spring. Retaining walls are bordered by white Indica azaleas trimmed as hedges.*

FOLLOWING PAGES: *The small garden is enclosed on three sides by stone walls thirteen feet in height. The fourth wall is the rear of the house with doors opening onto the garden, tying the two elements inextricably together.*

# Bankshaven

ometimes people visiting the South for the first time are surprised to discover that most private gardens are not as grand as the public ones associated with the region. Of course there are exceptions. Notable among these are the gardens at Bankshaven, the country estate of William Nathaniel Banks near Newnan, Georgia.

The original plan for the gardens was designed in 1929 by eminent landscape architect William C. Pauley, who allowed much of the 300-acre site to remain natural with its abundance of oaks, pines and poplars. His design included a sparkling brook-fed lake and five primary planting areas: a fountain garden, a formal walled flower garden, a swimming pool and pavilion, a boxwood garden with gazebo and finally, the lawn and plantings leading down to the lake.

The gardens are kept much as architect Pauley intended. According to Banks, the design of the landscaping at Bankshaven has "inevitability." There's a logic and cohesion to it all that allows the viewer to anticipate what is to come. The next view may be startling, but never out of context with other elements of the design.

The fountain garden was inspired by a beautiful Italian fountain carved of Carrara marble in the 1840's for an estate in north Georgia. Its three tiers of lions' masks and dolphins spout water, adding the dimension of sound to a garden where scent and sight are all-pervasive. In this setting, borders of boxwoods are filled with white Triumphator tulips each spring, followed by white impatiens that bloom throughout the summer months.

Beyond the boxwood garden, an ivy-covered wall surrounds the formal garden, which fairly shouts with exuberance. Here there are five central beds with roses, five with peonies and three with chrysanthemums, all bordered by narcissus. There are flowers in this garden from early spring until the first frost.

Magnificent border beds displaying flowers that bloom in succession from March until November run all along the walled formal garden. Beginning in early spring a host of daffodils, red and yellow tulips, blue Dutch irises and yellow and blue violas bloom beneath pink and white dogwoods and flowering fruit trees. By the first of May, when the peonies and roses are in bloom, the beds boast foxgloves, sweet williams and early daisies. Summer brings white phlox, blue stokesia, white lilies, yellow daylilies, marigolds, white and pink astilbe, zinnias and sultana, plus coreopsis and bee-balm surrounded with a blue ageratum border.

In early fall, yellow and white chrysanthemums replace the annuals. As the season ends, beds are mulched and several thousand bulbs are added in anticipation of spring and the gardens' annual rite of renewal.

Bankshaven's climax and central feature is the great expanse of manicured lawn bordered by shrubbery on both sides that stretches from the back of the house to the edge of a 10-acre lake. Peacocks strut on the lawn, while ducks, geese and swans glide upon the clear lake. Ancient white oaks and pines, wild azaleas, honeysuckles and camellias blooming in the surrounding woods complete a setting that knows no peer.

PRECEDING PAGES: *Tall cherry laurels shade a boxwood-bordered path leading to an intricately designed gazebo.*

LEFT AND ABOVE: *An abundance of foxgloves, violas, daylilies and 'Betty Prior' roses blooms in beds and along paths in the large formal garden at Bankshaven.*

ABOVE: *Ivy-covered brick walls surround the formal garden where hundreds of colorful tulips and Dutch irises bloom each spring.*

FACING PAGE: *A graceful three-tiered fountain of Carrara marble, carved in Italy in 1840 for an estate in north Georgia, is prominently displayed in a circular garden of stately boxwoods.*

ABOVE: *A marble statue depicting spring, carved in Italy about 1840, is surrounded by brilliant crimson azaleas.*

FACING PAGE: *A large double doorway with magnificent fanlight reveals a sweeping expanse of lawn bordered on both sides by shrubbery that leads to the lake beyond.*

# Milburne

Milburne, a stately Georgian mansion in Richmond, built in 1934 by Mr. and Mrs. Walter S. Robertson, Sr., is situated on a beautifully wooded bluff overlooking Virginia's James River. The five-acre site is located at the end of Lock Lane, named long ago when it was a simple path leading to one of the locks on the Kanawha Canal.

The house, designed by eminent New York architect William Lawrence Bottomly, is distinguished for its simplicity and elegance. Bottomly worked closely with landscape architect Charles F. Gillette, with whom he collaborated for over a decade, to arrive at the proper fusion of house and grounds. Together they achieved a rare expression of the Georgian spirit within a Virginia tradition in gardening.

At the entrance, 9-foot brick piers forming the gate are surmounted by molded urns chosen to complement the brick wall that encloses the front greensward. Bottomly planned the circular driveway with its center oblong lawn for ease of movement and harmony of style. To establish symmetry, Gillette chose four tulip poplars that stand like sentinels at even intervals along each side of the green and two white dogwoods at either end to ease the rigidity. For the forecourt, Bottomly designed a cobblestone and Belgian-block courtyard displaying a stone compass as its central medallion, the essential landscape symbol for space and movement within the entrance area and gardens.

To appease his fondness for freedom in plant materials, Gillette planted a "Wild Garden" north of the house. Brick steps lead up to the wilderness allowing the casual stroller to wend his way along a brick-edged pine straw path through a woodland area planted with periwinkle, Japanese holly, American holly, 6-foot azaleas of mixed color and variety, ferns, magnolias, Virginia pines, camellias and irises.

At the east end of the house is the parterre garden with designs marked in English boxwood clipped and shaped in arabesque precision. An air of cool elegance is achieved with white azaleas, wisteria and geraniums. The essential feature is the surrounding balustrade of cast stone designed after one at Hatfield House outside London, childhood home of Queen Elizabeth I.

Through her involvement with the Garden Club of Virginia, Mrs. Robertson met Arthur Surcliffe, well-known landscapist to Colonial Williamsburg. It was he who planned the expanse of lawn retained at the bluff by a curved brick wall, open at the center with wrought iron, to allow full advantage of the view.

In 1943, a devastating fire wiped out the woodlands below the balustrade. When the ash cooled, the Robertsons began replanting pines, oaks, hollies and mountain laurels determined to recreate their effect. Within a few years the growth had become so lush that landscape architect Umberto Innocenti recommended removing several large trees and planting mimosas on each side to softly frame the space. Courageously, Mrs. Robertson followed his advice, creating one of the most spectacular views of the river in Richmond.

The Bottomly-Gillette gardens have become a palette of color and design. Few Tidewater gardens equal those at Milburne for their expression of Georgian dignity and natural beauty.

PRECEDING PAGES: *Enormous oak trees shade the manicured lawn which is framed on either side by a plantation of boxwoods, American hollies and magnolias. A brick wall, pierced in the center by delicate wrought iron, affords a spectacular view of the James River.*

LEFT: *The stately mansion, designed by William Lawrence Bottomly, is an outstanding example of Georgian architecture. An unusual cast stone balustrade enclosing the formal "white" garden was designed by Alden Hopkins after one at Hatfield House, girlhood home of Queen Elizabeth I of England.*

ABOVE: *Brick steps lead to a pine straw path in the "Wild Garden" designed by Richmond, Virginia, landscape architect Charles F. Gillette. Plants in the area include periwinkle, azaleas, iris and camellias.*

ABOVE: *A swath of green grass centers the small, formal garden where white tulips, peonies and azaleas bloom each spring within a brick-edged border.*

FACING PAGE: *Mature trees lend dignity to the boxwood parterre garden where large Oriental vessels planted with white geraniums, accent the corners.*

# Touch of Normandy

Inspiration for this picturesque manor house and courtyard garden was drawn from Normandy in northwestern France. Its architect, Aymar Embury, was stationed there during World War I and stayed on after the war to study the architecture of the buildings typical of the area.

Early in the 1930's after he returned to the States and began his architectural career, a college friend from Princeton called to ask that he design a house for him. The friend had seen a number of the architect's designs and felt that Embury could produce exactly what he wanted. There were only three specific requests: a vaulted ceiling in the living room, variations in room elevations and somewhere in the design, a turreted tower to resemble an ancient keep. Aside from these requests, Embury was given carte blanche to site the house and gardens on a 10-acre tract of land, and his design does indeed evoke images of Normandy.

From the entrance in a surrounding wall, the driveway leads through a small park to a walled courtyard enclosing the front of the house. Here, a small rose garden is an integral part of the overall plan.

For years the original owners worked diligently to maintain the garden exactly as the architect planned. But as time passed, the trees in the park area grew to great heights and cast long, beautiful shadows across the courtyard . . . shadows that unfortunately discouraged good growth for roses.

Some ten years ago, the house changed hands, moving from one generation to the next as the daughter and her family assumed possession. She, being as dedicated a Francophile and as enthusiastic a gardener as her parents, tried valiantly to maintain the rose garden strictly as such, but after a few disappointing seasons began to consider the possibility of adding plants more tolerant to filtered light.

Through trial and error, she discovered a new dimension in gardening: hydrangeas, peonies and daisies brought a welcome palette of blue and white to the predominantly pink array. Unwilling to give up completely on roses, she searched until she finally found an old-fashioned variety called 'Betty Prior' that is hardy and grows well in semishade.

Beginning with the first warm days of spring, blue and white pansies are placed in the border as early bulbs begin to emerge and herald the season. Summer marks the height as roses, hydrangeas, peonies and daisies all bloom in an opulent display of pastel color. As fall comes slowly south, lavender chrysanthemums replace the summer flowers and bloom along with the faithful 'Betty Prior' roses until November. Occasionally, a replacement chrysanthemum or zinnia is transferred from a large holding bed to the ''prima donna'' courtyard area for additional color as the season wanes. But winter is left as Nature intended, neat but bare, in anticipation of the next season.

On a recent trip through France, new inspiration from the pastoral countryside found its way back home. An apple orchard in the park and a trellis placed against the tower for wisteria add still another touch of Normandy.

FACING PAGE: *A variety of flowering plants and shrubs such as hydrangeas, roses, pink and white impatiens and daisies blooms in this courtyard garden. Wisteria and roses climbing on a lattice panel and watermelon pink crape myrtle blooming against weathered stucco walls of the turret are reminiscent of the French countryside.*

ABOVE: *Walls decorated with ivy swags and brick piers topped by stone fruit baskets distinguish the entrance to the cobblestone courtyard and garden of the house.*

ABOVE: *Towering pines, oaks and magnolias in the entrance park are visible above the forecourt.*

FACING PAGE: *The entrance to the house, silhouetted against 'Betty Prior' roses, features a foundation planting of two types of liriope. Decorative fretwork containers hold ligustrum and roses frame the front door.*

# Renaissance Vision

According to well-known British landscaper Robin Loder, "A view is worth a thousand blooms; a lake is worth ten thousand." When a *view* and a *lake* combine with tens of thousands of blossoms and the magnificence of mature trees, the visual pleasure can be great. Such a rare combination of landscaping features is brought together in the 22-acre estate situated on a wooded hillside near Baltimore, Maryland.

In fact, the garden is so ethereal, so inspiring, it is difficult to believe that it is located anywhere in North America. Italy — or France, perhaps — where sumptuous grandeur and opulence in garden design were the pleasures of kings and potentates . . . but Baltimore?

Actually, inspiration for the garden came from the Italian Villa d'Este, in Tivoli. When Philadelphia landscape architect Arthur F. Paul was commissioned to design the garden 40 years ago for previous owners, he found a wooded ravine behind the house the perfect setting for a series of stairways, terraces and fountains reminiscent of the main axis at the Villa d'Este. It is this view, running north and cut through woodland, that the British would probably consider worth one hundred thousand blossoms, rather than just a mere thousand.

The view begins at the rear of the house and starts down a flight of horseshoe stairs into a formal boxwood garden, then descends a steep incline by means of a stone stairway that cuts sharply through the trees to a stream far below. The edges of the stairway are planted with beautiful flowering dogwoods, mountain laurels, magnolias and rhododendrons, creating a flowering allée. The branches of tall deciduous trees — maples, tulip poplars and ash — arch high overhead forming a verdant canopy. Beyond a bridge over the stream, the stone stairs ascend a steep incline, with terraces at strategic places, featuring gushing fountains. Finally, at the crest of the ascent, the vista culminates in a magnificent swan fountain set in the middle of an amphitheater of tall cedar trees.

The lake is the focal point of another spectacular vista. This view, from the main house, is west across a park-like meadow, down a gentler slope to the shore of the lake. Here, the spacious expanses of grass are punctuated by majestic tulip trees towering into heights of more than 60 feet. In spring, the edges of the encroaching woodland sparkle with myriad blossoms from native dogwoods, redbuds and horse chestnuts.

Blossoms begin in early spring with drifts of daffodils sweeping down grassy slopes to the lakeshore, followed by massed plantings of white and pink azaleas. Wisteria vines scramble over stone archways, and climbing hydrangeas festoon the walls of the main house. Wildflowers bejewel the woodland floor — blue phlox, spring beauty and May apples galore — flowering, setting seed and storing energy even before the leaves of the trees are mature.

Trees give the estate character and a sense of maturity, and the owner worries each time there is a storm. "I don't think I could bear to lose one," she says. "People think that my garden is so special because of the main vista, but nothing impresses me so much as the trees."

FACING PAGE: *A series of fountains accents the vista where tiered steps lead to the main house. Inspiration for the garden came from the famous Italian Villa d'Este in Tivoli. The walkways and steps are edged with azaleas, dogwoods, rhododendrons and spiraling cedars.*

ABOVE: *A massive wall containing a stone arch is draped in wisteria and lilacs. The arch gives access to a secluded Blue Garden, where all the flowers are predominantly shades of blue and white.*

ABOVE: *Looking from the main house across a greensward are giant tulip poplars which frame yet another vista to a lake beyond.*

FACING PAGE: *Viewed from a balcony of the house, the main vista is breathtaking in early spring. A boxwood hedge encloses this lawn, and beyond, decends into a valley which is dissected by a stream. Steps continue up the other side in tiers, each with a fountain, ascending to an amphitheater formed by a semicircle of towering cedar trees.*

# Planned Perfection

Talented landscape designer Jim Gibbs believes in the adage Timing is everything. His decision to move to Atlanta, Georgia, a city he had long admired for its topographical beauty and moderate climate, coincided with a residential building boom . . . a fortunate bit of timing for a man whose profession is designing, planting and maintaining gardens.

Gibbs' gardens agree in style and character with the architecture of the houses they embellish and are designed to extend the boundaries both visually and practically. His plans include well-defined walkways connecting the house and garden, walls and fences framing the property and providing background for flowering shrubs and ornaments; different levels add dimension to the overall landscape design.

Garden planning can be compared to the construction and decoration of a house. Where houses have rooms with walls, ceilings and floors, garden perimeters extend from sky to ground. Both designate areas for entertaining, relaxing and playing that are furnished with such accoutrements as chairs, benches and art objects. Just as a decorator chooses wall coverings and materials with eye appeal and durability, landscapers select plants to enhance and augment the exterior.

Gibbs, owner of Gibbs Landscape Company in Atlanta, and his family make their home in a formal Williamsburg residence. The landscaper began designing the garden after the house was built in 1971. His plan required patience; it called for a new phase to be installed each year over a five-year period. When he had finished, the setting had become a world unto itself, an environment that unfolds and presents a different and surprising view at every turn.

The 125- by 200-foot plot is comprised of three levels connected by a series of steps. The first phase of the five-year plan saw completion of grading for all three planned levels. A ground cover was established, and all understory trees, cherry, dogwood and crape myrtle were planted. These secondary flowering trees planted beneath towering pines introduce a human scale, important to the overall balance of the garden. The second year, brick replaced the grass paths. These handsome brick walkways feature a running bond pattern with a header course and a soldier course border. The walkways' strong directional lines lead the wanderer from one level to the next and promote a sense of flow. The third year, brick columns and a cedar fence encircled the space, while the fourth called for a Buckingham slate terrace adjacent to the house that was covered by an arbor to be enclosed. The arbor was moved and serves as a focal point for the lower level. It is strategically located to furnish a perfect spot for viewing all three levels in several directions.

The grounds are planted with geraniums, lilies, English ivy, crape myrtle and English boxwood. For emphasis, Gibbs added a sprinkling of unusual trees, including a 35-year-old Japanese threadleaf Dissectum maple, a rare golden chain tree, a multi-trunk Washington Hawthorn, and a 30-year-old tree-form camellia.

Now that every phase of the plan is completed, Gibbs and his family enjoy the fruits of their labor in a garden where colors, textures, heights and shapes bring visual pleasure to every season.

PRECEDING PAGES: *The statue of Leda overlooks a formal English boxwood garden displaying a golden chain tree and a prize Washington Hawthorn tree. Vodka begonias add vivid color in the rectangular beds. Iron Baronet settees at either end were made by Fisk Ironworks in New York.*

FACING PAGE: *Tall pines and an understory of dogwoods and other flowering trees furnish a background in this garden. A curved brick walk framed by English ivy, creates a strong directional line and leads the eye to a stone statue of Leda. A crape myrtle tree stands opposite an antique urn containing red geraniums.*

ABOVE: *A low-branched dogwood and a Kwansan cherry tree frame the view of a stone statue on the lower level. Magnolias in the background provide weight and balance.*

FOLLOWING PAGE: *An architectural mound was constructed on the lower level of the garden to interrupt a flat expanse of lawn. Blue rug junipers, white begonias, red geraniums and variegated English hollies surround a small stone statue. The wisteria-covered arbor offers a view in several directions.*

# Public Gardens

# Biltmore

The gardens of Biltmore House, the immense Vanderbilt-owned estate near Asheville, North Carolina, exhibit the grand and graceful achievement of the 19th century landscape master Frederick Law Olmstead.

Young George Vanderbilt engaged Olmstead to create the proper setting for his château while it was being designed by Richard Morris Hunt. Vanderbilt could easily afford the finest in landscaping, and Olmstead was the logical choice, with New York City's Central Park and other outstanding urban parks and estates to his credit.

Developing a scheme for the estate became Olmstead's greatest challenge. Farmers and loggers had previously abused and impoverished the land, but Olmstead was undaunted by the extensive soil renewal that was required. He conceived a plan for the gardens surrounding the palatial home that dazzles the imagination. Rare and unusual trees were ordered from the best American and European nurseries. Evergreens including exotic spruces, cedars, hollies, yews and pines were interplanted with hardwoods such as beeches, oaks, hickories, firs and basswoods. Native rhododendron and numerous flowering trees — cherry, magnolia, dogwood, tulip, silverbell and crab apple — were also purchased.

When the time came to implement this extensive theme, Olmstead sent for Chauncey Delos Beadle, a landscaper who had been educated at Cornell and was working in New York. Beadle became foreman of the operation and established nurseries to sustain the young trees until they were ready to be set into place. It took a thousand men five years to construct the château and complete the necessary large-scale growing and planting. When the gardens were finished, Vanderbilt persuaded Beadle to accept a permanent position as superintendent of the grounds and nurseries. He remained at the estate until his death 50 years later.

During the 1930's, an important association, which became known as the "Azalea Hunters," was formed. The group included Beadle, his chauffeur Sylvester Owens and two Asheville men, Dr. William A. Knight and Frank Creighton. Together they combed the forests of the Southeast looking for rare shrubs, trees and wild azaleas which could be transplanted in the estate gardens.

Strollers along the various walks at Biltmore encounter a succession of breathtaking scenes. The Azalea Gardens contain such rarities as the Florida Torreya, Florida Yew, Bigleaf and Ashe's magnolias and Elliottia, in addition to acres of native azaleas. Both common and exotic varieties reach a glorious peak in the month of May. A few steps away is the English Walled Garden, filled with vast armies of roses and formal beds of tulips, chrysanthemums and various perennials and annuals, all superb in their seasons.

Just below the mansion stretches the formal expanse of the Italian Garden with its pools of water plants separated by manicured lawn panels, reminiscent of gardens in the great European cities. The placement of clipped hemlock hedges and Italian statuary completes the effect.

In every season Biltmore House offers much to admire for anyone who appreciates beauty. The splendor of these gardens is the fulfillment of far-sighted men of a different time.

ABOVE: *Situated high on a hill near Asheville, North Carolina, Biltmore House commands a sweeping view of the surrounding countryside. The 250-room mansion reflects Francis I style French 16th century château. Evergreens including exotic spruces, cedars, yews, and pines are interspersed with hardwoods such as beech, oak, hickory, fir and basswood.*

FACING PAGE: *Tulips present a lavish display of color in the four-acre Walled Garden. Over 50,000 bulbs are planted every fall to provide the biggest and best blooms for spring.*

FOLLOWING PAGES: *Tulips are planted in large geometric beds in front of the conservatory. Spring flowers are replaced with roses in summer and chrysanthemums in fall along with various perennials and annuals.*

ABOVE: *Rays of the morning sun pierce the mist to shine on pale pink wild azaleas (Rhododendron canescens) brought from the high mountains of the Blue Ridge.*

FACING PAGE: *The Azalea Garden is dedicated to former gardens Superintendent Chauncey Beadle, who spent 10 years searching the swamps, hills, and plains of America for specimens of native azaleas.*

FOLLOWING PAGES: *Native pink and white dogwoods and azaleas along with numerous other varieties, are planted along pathways and among the towering white pines. Due to the diverse plantings, blooms can be found from April until mid-summer. The most spectacular display, however, occurs around the first week of May.*

# Middleton Place

Ten miles west of Charleston, South Carolina, the Ashley River is a symphony of graceful, sweeping curves before its final confluence with the Cooper River and entrance to the sea. This is Carolina Low Country — mostly flat and swampy. But at a point of high ground on the south bank, at Middleton Place Plantation, is one of the world's most beautiful landscaped gardens.

In the late 17th century, the plantation was acquired as dowry by Henry Middleton when he married Mary Williams. For more than a century it remained the family seat for generations of distinguished Middletons: Henry, president of the First Continental Congress; Arthur, a signer of the Declaration of Independence; Henry, legislator, Governor of South Carolina and U.S. minister to Russia; and Williams, who signed the Ordinance of Secession five years before the Civil War consumed Middleton Place and almost brought about its total destruction.

The main house, an imposing early Jacobean-style mansion of red brick, was burned by Union troops in 1865 and the ruins were leveled 21 years later by an earthquake. Only the south flanker remained intact. The gardens lay overgrown and neglected until early in this century, when the late J. J. Pringle Smith, a direct descendant of Henry Middleton, and his wife, Heningham Lyons Ellett, spent years restoring and embellishing the house and gardens. This achievement was nationally recognized in 1941 when The Garden Club of America awarded Middleton Place the Bulkley Medal "in commemoration of 200 years of enduring beauty."

Charles Duell, the eighth generation to act as steward of Middleton, carries on the gardening tradition. The gardens of this 110-acre historic landmark feature several informal areas, but at their heart they reflect a classic French style of landscaping. Rational order, formality and symmetrical views with specific focal points are integrated into the design. Terraces in front of the house descend to a pair of lakes designed in the shape of a butterfly that spread out below at river level. A reflecting pool planted with azaleas and shrubs is graced by a family of swans. Small gardens made private by hedges of azaleas enclose seating accommodations for quiet contemplation.

A nineteenth-century expansion of the gardens reflected the British trend toward naturalism: winding paths cut through woodland, azaleas informally planted along slopes and pathways, and ponds created with irregular shorelines. Natural areas surround the formal part of the gardens, with ponds, lakes and bridges helping to effect a smooth transition.

Tradition suggests that as a result of his friendship with the family, the notable French botanist André Michaux visited Middleton Place in 1786 and brought with him camellias, the first to be planted in America. Some of the original plants still survive and flower each spring.

Despite its turbulent past, Middleton Place is today a haven of peace and tranquility. It is a world long vanished from the American scene — rich in history, designed for a life of elegance and gentility, where the haunting cry of the domesticated peacock and the clack-clack of the wild heron are nature's enduring song.

LEFT: *A rustic arched bridge spans Rice Mill Pond, connecting the formal area of the gardens with a wooded hillside planted with thousands of naturalized pink and red azaleas. Wisteria and wild Cherokee roses cascading from treetops appear brilliant against the gray melancholy of surrounding savannahs.*

ABOVE: *Wild roses climb a moss-draped oak at the foot of Azalea Hill.*

FOLLOWING PAGES: *Azalea Hill meets the irregular shoreline of Rice Mill Pond where pennyweed, gatorweed and duckweed flourish.*

ABOVE: *Situated on a bluff overlooking the Ashley River, a portion of the octagonal garden is bordered in bright yellow pansies.*

RIGHT: *The original Middleton Place house, built about 1755, was a central structure with two connecting wings. In 1865, all but the existing wing was destroyed by Union troops. The gardens were planned on an axis from the front door of the first house to a bend in the nearby Ashley River.*

# Orton

The grandeur of the Old South lives on at Orton Plantation Gardens, where moss-draped oaks border garden walks and complement carefully placed annuals and flowering shrubs. Located on the west bank of the Cape Fear River between Wilmington and Southport, North Carolina, the estate boasts a past as colorful as the flowers that bloom there.

During the late 1600's and early 1700's pirates and Indians stalked the area, which acquired its forbidding name after numerous vessels ran afoul of the treacherous shoals offshore. Colonel Maurice Moore, who once vanquished the fearsome pirate Captain Edward "Blackbeard" Teach, originally owned the Orton land. In the intervening years Orton had an array of owners.

After the War Between the States, the estate remained vacant and rapidly deteriorated. Fortunately, Colonel K. M. Murchison bought it in 1884 and spent enormous sums of money rehabilitating the plantation, successfully retrieving its lost splendor. When the Colonel died in 1904, a son-in-law, James Sprunt, bought the property as a gift for his wife Luola. It was she who began developing the gardens. When their son James Laurence Sprunt inherited Orton in 1924 he continued his mother's horticultural work.

Landscape architect Robert Swann Sturtevant designed many areas; others were masterminded by Churchill Bragaw, who managed the estate during the 1930's when it was first opened to the public. James Laurence Sprunt's son Kenneth and his family now maintain the gardens as a tribute to his parents.

Much of the plantation's charm comes from the surrounding lakes and lagoons. Hundreds of large camellias interspersed with Kurume and Indian azaleas are mirrored in the water. Flowering peach, cherry and apple trees along with *Daphne odora* and winter and summer annuals add variety and contrast. A number of old oaks are festooned with wisteria and Cherokee roses, and an arbor is covered in Banksia roses.

One particularly noteworthy section is the Scroll Garden, where curving podocarpus hedges surround numerous geometric flower beds as well as larger, more flowing designs. Two wooden structures with lattice-like sides that resemble small seaside piers are at opposite ends of the parterre and afford visitors a view of lagoons dotted with swamp cypress. Many of the fields where rice grew in years gone by are put to good use by the State of North Carolina, which leases them for bird sanctuaries.

The neck of the largest lake is crossed by a Chinese-style zig-zag bridge, designed to thwart pursuing evil spirits, which the ancient Chinese believed could travel only in a straight line.

Mother Nature is not always predictable, but if she is kind, January through February brings camellias, daphne and ardisia; March through April finds azaleas, camellias, wisteria, Indian hawthornes, dogwoods, Cherokee and Banksia roses, pansies and flowering fruit trees in grand numbers. Daylilies, pansies, oleanders, hydrangeas, rhododendrons, gardenias, water lilies, magnolias and irises are in full array during May and June. Summer annuals, crape myrtles and water lilies bloom from June through September, bringing year-round beauty to Orton.

PRECEDING PAGES: *Orton House, the Sprunts' private home, provides a picturesque backdrop for the surrounding lawns and gardens.*

FACING PAGE: *Cypress and live oak trees provide a complementary setting for azaleas and other ornamentals flowering near the lagoon.*

ABOVE: *A lagoon reflects the soft shades of azaleas and Chinese wisteria.*

LEFT: *The terrace path overlooks the Scroll Garden where curving podocarpus hedges surround beds of annuals. Beyond are the old rice fields, now a wildlife sanctuary.*

FOLLOWING PAGES: *The crooked bridge over the water garden is based on Chinese walkways built in a zig-zag configuration to foil pursuing evil spirits who, according to ancient Chinese legend, could only travel in straight lines.*

# Elizabethan

In 1587, several decades before Jamestown and Plymouth Rock, a group of English settlers landed on Roanoke Island in what is now North Carolina. Soon after their arrival, two of these brave travelers, Ananias and Elinor Dare had a daughter, Virginia, who was the first English child born in America. Her grandfather and leader of the group, John White, sailed back to England for supplies. When he returned, the colonists had completely disappeared. Only a single clue was left behind: the word "Croatan" carved on a tree. The mystery concerning the disappearance of these New World settlers has never been explained.

Elizabethan Gardens, established by the Garden Club of North Carolina as a memorial to the attempted colonization under Elizabeth I, is located on the island where the puzzling and tragic story of the Lost Colony took place. Inspired by the gift of some rare statuary from the estate of The Honorable John Hay Whitney, Ambassador to the Court of St. James, and Mrs. Whitney, the gardens were planned and erected by the renowned landscape firm of Innocenti & Webel. Appropriately, the 10-acre, $250,000 setting opened in 1960 on the 373rd anniversary of the birth of Virginia Dare.

The iron gates of the impressive entrance wall once hung at the French Embassy in Washington; the wall itself is constructed of warm, pinkish-brown handmade brick dating from the late 1800's. The same handmade brick was used to construct the gatehouse, which is furnished with rare antiques, gifts to the Garden Club from members and interested friends.

These year-round gardens have won enthusiastic praise from visitors from all over the world. Camellias are featured through the fall and winter, and in the spring, masses of blooming dogwoods, azaleas, bulbs, flowering fruit trees and spring annuals greet visitors. The cloistered Queen's Rose Garden, designed by the English landscape architect Lewis Clarke, reigns supreme in May and continues to bloom through October. Summer brings magnolias, gardenias, crape myrtle, day lilies, hybrid lilies and bedding plants. Beneath the gnarled branches of the ancient trees, lady slippers, pitcher plants, foam flowers and ferns may be found in unexpected spots. Other unusual features include an authentic 16th century gazebo and a Shakespearean herb garden.

An antique Pompeian fountain and pool with carved stone balustrade from the Whitney collection constitute the central focal point of the Sunken Garden. The coat-of-arms on the balustrade is that of the powerful Farnesi family of 16th century Italy, an insigne which may bind the fountain to the sculptor Michelangelo, who contributed his efforts to the Farnesi Palace near Rome. The fountain is surrounded by parterre beds filled with blooming plants and outlined in clipped helleri holly. The entire area is enclosed by a low perforated wall of old handmade brick and an eleven-foot high pleached allée of native yaupon holly featuring 32 arched openings.

Much attention has been given to the authenticity of numerous features to be found in these North Carolina gardens. Elizabethan in style and spirit yet adapted to the present, the setting provides an outstanding example of excellence in horticulture and landscape architecture.

FACING PAGE: *An avenue of yaupons and great oaks leads to a statue of Virginia Dare which was carved from Carrara marble in 1859 by Louisa Lander of Salem, Massachusetts.*

ABOVE: *This twin oak in The Elizabethan Gardens near Manteo, North Carolina, is believed to have been standing at the time colonists arrived on Roanoke Island in 1587.*

RIGHT: *The Gatehouse, modeled after a 16th century orangery, is furnished with rare antiques donated to The Garden Club of North Carolina. In summer, the parterre gardens are filled with bright yellow marigolds and accented with geraniums, dahlias and crape myrtles.*

ABOVE: *The Sunken Garden features beds outlined in clipped helleri holly and filled with blooming plants. It is surrounded by an 11-foot-high pleached allée of native yaupon holly.*

FACING PAGE: *The focal point of the Sunken Garden is an antique Pompeian fountain and pool with carved stone balustrade from the estate of John Hay Whitney.*

# Winterthur

In 1969, after the death of Henry F. du Pont, C. Gordon Tyrrell, an Englishman and then director of Du Pont's Winterthur Gardens, wrote that it was probably more English than any other garden, including many in Great Britain itself. The 1,000-acre estate of gently rolling hills is located just 6 miles north of Wilmington, Delaware.

The Winterthur estate dates back to 1839, when James A. Bidermann and his wife Evalina built their home just a few miles from the Du Pont company's gunpowder mills on Brandywine River. She was the daughter of Éleuthère Irénée du Pont de Nemours, the French aristocrat who fled the French Revolution to found a chemical dynasty in America. As soon as their home was completed, the Bidermanns built a formal sunken garden at the rear of the house. They named the estate Winterthur after a town in Switzerland where Mr. Bidermann's family had lived.

In 1902, Colonel Henry A. du Pont, a nephew of Mrs. Bidermann, made the estate his home and enlarged the garden. The Colonel's son, Henry F. du Pont, grew up with a fondness for gardening, and while a schoolboy turned his attention to planting masses of flowering bulbs at the edges of the lawns and in the woods. His skill in blending flowers with the natural landscape produced breathtaking effects. He thought in terms of color and form, and he created bold plantings.

Henry F. du Pont's love of trees knew no limits; he once told his staff in the event of fire, "just be sure you wet down the trees. I can replace the house, but I can't replace the trees." He had a tree surgeon rout out the diseased wood of one old sycamore and then had 16 tons of concrete poured inside the trunk to fill the enormous cavity. Today, more than 20 years later, the tree is thriving.

Mr. du Pont followed three guidelines in laying out his garden: bold arrangement of plants in large masses, coordinating plants with the terrain and meticulous attention to companion planting to achieve exciting colors.

Over 150 varieties of daffodils cover 10 acres of open hillsides. An impressive azalea collection began in 1915 when Mr. du Pont bought seventeen Kurume azaleas exhibited by the Japanese at the San Francisco Exposition. He propagated them by taking hundreds of cuttings and planting them throughout his woods. Today, azaleas are scattered throughout the gardens and grounds, but the most impressive displays are in the Azalea Woods. Each color and variety is carefully placed to draw visitors along pathways.

Each season at Winterthur brings a new spectacle of color. September sees the hillsides covered with beautiful colchicums with large lavender flowers. Because of the extensive woodland and Mr. du Pont's careful selection of shrubs for fall color, October can be the most colorful of all months . . . the trees aglow in fiery red, burnished bronze and buttercup yellow. Yet the depths of winter, too, can be hauntingly beautiful. Under the blanket of snow, tiny bulbs lie dormant, ready for spring to renew the extravaganza of color.

"A beautiful garden I think of as being a work of art," wrote Henry F. du Pont, "but unlike a painting or book, a garden grows and always changes." Winterthur Gardens are the magnum opus of a devoted artist.

PRECEDING PAGES: *Henry Francis du Pont's extraordinary legacy includes 200 landscaped acres, rolling meadows and untouched woodlands. Masses of colchicum, also called autumn crocus, have been naturalized across an entire hillside at Winterthur.*

ABOVE: *Along paths in the Azalea Woods, pink rhododendrons are interplanted with shrubs such as viburnum, also called Chinese snowball.*

FACING PAGE: *The Sundial Garden, surrounded by English boxwoods, is planted with a rich array of flowering trees — dogwoods, ornamental cherries, crab apples, lilacs, quince, and spirea.*

FOLLOWING PAGES: *Daffodils, planted in drifts, cover open hillsides in March and April. Varieties with stiff stems and upward facing flowers were selected because they bloom longer and multiply each year.*

# Longue Vue

ongue Vue, called one of America's greatest city estate gardens, consists of one large garden surrounded by six smaller ones, each different in color and design. Situated on an eight-acre tract in the heart of New Orleans, Louisiana, Longue Vue was developed by Mr. and Mrs. Edgar B. Stern, based on a plan designed by the well-respected landscape architect Ellen B. Shipman.

The house is approached along a two-hundred-foot long allée of live oaks pruned into a cathedral arch, beneath which grows a ground cover of vinca major and Confederate jasmine. The entrance court is paved in a geometric pattern of granite block brought from Europe as ship's ballast in the 19th century.

The first area to be cultivated was the Wild Garden. Once an empty stretch of lawn, it is now planted with flowering trees and shrubs indigenous to the Gulf Coast. Some species found here are *Magnolia grandiflora*, the state flower of both Louisiana and Mississippi, dogwoods, oak-leaf hydrangeas, wild azaleas, camellias, viburnum, sweet olives and mountain laurels.

Over the years, the Walled Garden has evolved from a vegetable plot to a permanent home for three varieties of floribunda roses: a red 'Europeana,' a yellow 'Sun Sprite' and an orange 'First Edition.'

The largest and most formal garden of the estate is the Spanish Court. Inspired by a visit to the Generalife Gardens in Grenada, Spain, Mrs. Stern asked landscape architect William Platt to create a similar setting at Longue Vue. The result is a combination Moorish-Spanish design with fountains, jardiniere planting and mosaic walks.

Further evidence of the European influence can be seen in the Canal Garden which resembles those in Lisbon, Portugal.

The Yellow Garden is a small patio area located near the guesthouse. It was designed by Mrs. Stern and is reminiscent of a garden she saw in England. Here variegated foliage, yellow flowering shrubs and vines grow around a fountain designed by Robert Engman of Pennsylvania. Such flowering shrubs as lantana and thryallis and vines of Carolina yellow jessamine, allamanda and stigma phyllon highlighted by seasonal yellow daffodils and tulips and annuals in containers give the garden its name.

The Pan Garden takes its name from a statue of the Greek god which is perched atop an Italian Renaissance fountain base. Pan was the mythological god of shepherds, trees and meadows. Permanent foundation planting of Japanese magnolias, sweet olives and loquats forms a background for the camellia 'Pink Perfection' and polyantha roses 'Margot Koster.' On each side of the fountain is the plant, brunfelsia, called 'Yesterday, Today and Tomorrow' because in the course of three days its blossoms turn from deep purple to lavender and finally, to white.

The Portico Garden is a formal English rose garden. Harewood trimmed into geometric designs is centered by large camellia 'Pink Perfection' with Peace rose standards at either end.

Longue Vue has been open to the public since 1969, and the many and varied designs have provided inspiration for garden enthusiasts and students over the years.

PRECEDING PAGES: *The Yellow Garden features golden-hued marigold blossoms around a gently flowing fountain, created especially for this quiet, secluded patio by Robert Engman of Philadelphia. Variegated foliage and yellow flowering shrubs and vines, contrasted with solid greens, give this garden its name.*

LEFT *The focal point of Longue Vue is the Spanish Court; its design inspired by Generalife Gardens in Grenada, Spain.*

ABOVE: *Featured in the Spanish Court is a water mobile sculpture by Lin Emery. Constructed of white bronze, this fountain is a fantasy named "Arabesque."*

ABOVE: *A bronze elfin statue crafted by Josephine Knoblock presides over the Pan Garden. White daisies and begonias accent the perennial shrubs in this secluded garden.*

FACING PAGE: *A terrace of roses overlooks the East Lawn. 'Lady Banksia' roses cling to weathered stuccoed walls. Other roses featured are 'Pristine' tree roses underplanted with white 'Summersnow' and apricot 'Margot Koster.'*

# Tryon Palace

The gardens of Tryon Palace in New Bern, North Carolina, are beautifully groomed examples of the transitional stage in gardening design from the 17th century Dutch-English school to the natural landscaping of the 18th century.

The original Palace was built in 1767-70 as a government house and residence for the Governor of the royal colony of North Carolina, William Tryon. It served in this capacity until the outbreak of the Revolutionary War in 1775, when it was accidentally destroyed by fire. The building was authentically restored on its original foundation in the 1950's by the Tryon Palace Commission with bequests of the late Mrs. James Edwin Latham, a native New Bernian.

Since no complete record of the garden plans was found, the Commission decided to create a setting constructed and planted to resemble those that flourished in 17th and 18th century England. This style of privy garden, enclosed with walls and gates to discourage trespassers, was designed to be viewed from the house and was often accessible only to its occupants. Typical examples of this garden style, the Green Garden and the Kellenberger Garden, flank Tryon Palace.

The Green Garden has trimmed hedges of dwarf yaupon shaped into interlocking scrolls between gravel walks. Four identical triangular beds alternating with the scrolls are edged in lavender cotton and filled with periwinkle. Topiary shrubs of cherry laurel mark the corners, and a sculptured hedge forms the surrounding walls. At the center is a limestone statue, "Boy with Grapes."

The Kellenberger Garden is named in honor of Mrs. Latham's daughter and son-in-law, the late Mr. and Mrs. John A. Kellenberger, who served for many years as chairman and treasurer of the Tryon Palace Commission. It is oblong, encircled with high walls of handmade brick, divided in halves by a path. Beside the walls, trellises covered in climbing Confederate jessamine, cruel vines, Carolina jessamine and pyracantha form a background for flower beds. On one side, an antique font stands in the center of four rectangular beds of colorful blooms bordered by germander, with a shaped yew tree in the center. On the other side of the path, four inside curved beds bordered with sweet alyssum are planted with flowers that change with the seasons.

The most elaborate of the Palace gardens is the walled Maude Moore Latham Memorial Garden. Here, clipped hedges of dwarf yaupon planted in graceful reverse-S curves border beds of colorful flowers. Intricate brick paths lead between the beds to an octagonal central pool. On one side, four Italian marble statues representing the four seasons stand against ivy covered walls. On the other, curved steps lead to a colonnaded pavilion of classical design. Additional gardens in the complex are Hawks Allée, the Pleached Allée and the Kitchen and Work gardens.

Tryon Palace and Gardens have received much high acclaim and many honors. Perhaps the most notable is the Crowninshield Award, which was presented to Mrs. Kellenberger in 1966. This coveted award, bestowed by the National Trust for Historic Preservation, recognizes superlative achievement in the preservation and interpretation of sites and buildings significant in American history.

PRECEDING PAGES: *In the Maude M. Latham Memorial Garden, parterres edged with clipped yaupon swirl around the central hexagonal fountain pool, and brick paths lead between flower-filled beds. Small topiaries of cherry laurel accent diamond-shaped designs edged with white candytuft.*

ABOVE: *The Green Garden is a feat of pruning, shearing and clipping of miniature hedges of yaupon shaped into interlocking scrolls. Four identical triangular beds, edged with lavender cotton, enclose periwinkle. At each corner are topiary shrubs of cherry laurel.*

RIGHT: *Carefully placed gates in the encircling wall of the Memorial Garden afford visitors a view of parterres planted in yellow and white pansies.*

ABOVE: *The Kellenberger Garden, like other Palace gardens of English design, is oblong in shape enclosed with high walls of handmade brick. Curved beds are planted with bright yellow chrysanthemums.*

RIGHT: *In the fall, brilliant shades of copper, rust and yellow chrysanthemums are on view in the Maude M. Latham Memorial Garden. Although some beds are diamond-shaped or octagonal, their edges are curved, as are those of the octagonal central pool. Paths of rosy pink stone wind between the beds.*

FOLLOWING PAGES: *Against encircling brick walls in the Memorial Garden, Italian statues representing the four seasons enhance the unrivaled scene of hundreds of spring tulips in full bloom.*

# Cypress

ick Pope, founder of Florida's Cypress Gardens, enjoys telling how he came to create such a beautiful attraction against impossible odds. Back in 1931, he was sitting in a New York publicity office dreaming of Florida when he chanced to pick up a glossy magazine with a pictorial feature on Magnolia Gardens and learned that it had been created from a swamp.

Although the Great Depression was in full swing, Pope packed in his job, bundled his belongings and family into a car, and headed south to Winter Haven, Florida, where he knew of a swamp on the shores of Lake Eloise. All it needed was a massive landscaping so Dick Pope acquired 16 acres of swamp and pitched in to make his dream a reality.

He hired 40 men at a dollar a day and, with the help and support of his wife, Julie, began the project as a private venture. The gardens opened to the public in 1936 after five years of grueling, backbreaking work.

Pope realized that if his labor of love was to attract enough paying customers to provide a living for his family, he needed two vital ingredients; plantings that gave year-round color and lots of publicity to attract tourists. He obtained year-round color by searching far and wide for exotic plant material, by using not only tropical plants indigenous to the area but also making contact with botanical gardens in other countries and introducing promising new plants never before tried in the region. And he broadened the appeal by including attention-getting water-ski shows, exotic birds, a zoo and gift shops.

Nothing in the area outshines the gardens for pure spectacle. The first portion resembles a tropical rain forest, with huge philodendron vines and other creepers climbing to the treetops. A hiking trail emerges from this jungle and continues over several bridges, curving gracefully across beautiful green lawns edged with beds of flowering annuals to the top of a hill crowned by a white gazebo.

Highlighting the botanical extravaganza are stately cypress trees, their branches festooned with garlands of Spanish moss. Also spectacular is an immense Indian banyan tree, its massive branches supported by brace roots which start off as string-like strands that grow to resemble tree trunks. Towering displays of bougainvillea and flame vines, supported by tall, sturdy poles more than 50 feet high are among the gardens' more flamboyant sights.

A recent major expansion called "Gardens of the World" features 13 areas representing the styles of different countries. Included are a Southern garden, an Oriental garden and an English rose garden that boasts 15,000 award-winning roses.

More than 100 flower beds are currently featured at the gardens. The beds are completely changed four to seven times a year to feature the most colorful and appropriate flowers for the particular season. In December and January, for example, the winding walkways are ablaze with some 25,000 red, white and pink poinsettias, followed by Easter lilies and flowering bulbs.

Cypress Gardens has grown from the original 16-acre tract to an area of more than 220 acres.

FACING PAGE: *'Margaret Bacon' bougainvillea, supported by 50-foot high poles, reaches almost to the treetops. Yellow calendulas bloom in the hedge-lined flower bed.*

ABOVE: *In the Gardens of the World section, more than 7000 gallons of water per minute cascade over falls and flow into a rocky stream bed bordered with plants native to the Mediterranean coast.*

ABOVE LEFT: *In the Oriental gardens, a large Buddha figure presides over a lagoon filled with giant victoria annual water lilies that are native to South America.*

ABOVE RIGHT: *Old-fashioned lavender bougainvillea accents this view of the Oriental gardens. A yellow Tabebuia provides a bright spot of color among the trees.*

RIGHT: *Reminiscent of the fountains of Rome, the Italian fountains of Cypress Gardens are decorated with handmade mosaic tiles.*

FACING PAGE: *Purple Princess flowers grow along the canals, and nearby flower-lined paths lead visitors from one garden to another.*

FOLLOWING PAGES: *The setting sun silhouettes moss-draped cypress trees growing in a garden lake.*

# Bayou Bend

In 1927 when Miss Ima Hogg and her brothers Will and Mike began developing Homewoods in Houston, Texas, they selected fourteen acres of untamed woodland on a curve of the Buffalo Bayou as the site for their home, which they would call Bayou Bend. Over the next forty years, Miss Hogg was instrumental in creating a series of formal gardens, actively participating in both landscape design and placement of trees and shrubs with untiring and devoted determination.

Her inspiration for the gardens began on a visit to the Vatican in Rome, where she saw marble statues of Clio and Euterpe. Visualizing the figures in her Texas garden, she asked for and received permission to have copies made. The Antonio Frilli Studio was commissioned for the task, and while there, Miss Hogg chanced to see a statue of Diana. Thinking her an ideal companion to the other goddesses, she arranged for all three to be reproduced in Carrara marble for Bayou Bend.

Upon returning to Houston, she employed competent landscape architects to implement a design in the shape of a cross. The statue of Diana and the house are at either end of the main axis, and Clio and Euterpe secure the crosspiece. Since then, Bayou Bend Gardens have grown to more than a half-dozen gardens arranged across the rolling Texas countryside. Clio, the Muse of History, is the focal point in a formal garden of parterre design, which found great popularity in England in the 1600's. Here patterns of clipped evergreens remain attractive year-round, and near perfection is reached in spring when beds of light pink 'Hortensia' and 'Lavender Beauty' azaleas bloom.

Across a vista, Euterpe, the Muse of Poetry and Music, cushioned in Kurume azaleas and ivy, stands looking toward the seated Clio.

The Diana Garden, with its splendid grass terraces designed for seating when used as an amphitheater, is the largest of the gardens. Here the statue of Diana, goddess of the Hunt and the Moon, beautifully framed by arcs of water jets, is poised amid trees, neatly clipped shrubs and pink and lilac azaleas.

The basic four elements of English garden design — trees, hedges, lawn and water — are manifest in the East Garden. Hedges of *Camellia japonica* backed by wax leaf ligustrum form a sylvan green backdrop for azaleas pruned in three tiers of differing varieties and shades of pink.

A woodland path leads to the White Garden on through ravines underplanted with shade-loving plants to the fanciful Butterfly Garden, which is laid out in the shape of the exquisitely patterned insect for which it is named. Azaleas in shades of pink and red surrounded by clipped boxwood form the wings, and muted brick is used for the body and antennae.

When Miss Hogg gave Bayou Bend to the Museum of Fine Arts of Houston, she entrusted the care of the Gardens to the membership of the River Oaks Garden Club with this gentle reminder: "A love affair with Nature is a rewarding experience. It gladdens the eye and replenishes the spirit . . . neither rainfall nor feeding can nourish plant life and flowering things like a gardener's words of praise and love."

Ima Hogg's love for Bayou Bend Gardens was the essential ingredient that makes them thrive.

PRECEDING PAGES: *Bayou Bend, formerly the home of Miss Ima Hogg, was given by her to The Museum of Fine Arts in Houston. Today, Bayou Bend Gardens are more than a half-dozen gardens arranged across fourteen acres of natural woods and ravines near Buffalo Bayou.*

LEFT: *In spring, a profusion of lavender azaleas and pink hydrangeas frames the fountain and pool near the statue of Diana for which the garden is named. Here grass terraces are spaced for seating when the garden becomes an amphitheater.*

ABOVE: *An Italian marble urn enhanced with graceful figures holds brilliant pink hydrangeas that bloom throughout the summer.*

PRECEDING PAGES: *Clio, Muse of History, presides in the formal garden of parterre design. Clipped evergreens surround small beds planted with Kurume hybrid azaleas, light pink 'Hortensia' and 'Lavender Beauty.'*

FACING PAGE: *Tucked among trees in the native woodlands is a ravine interplanted with ferns, aspidistra, saxifraga and other shade-loving plants.*

ABOVE: *In 1936, Miss Hogg envisioned a garden adapting the butterfly's wing pattern to an azalea bed. Principally using Kurume hybrid azaleas in shades of pink and red, surrounded by clipped boxwood in a parterre design for the wings, and soft pink brick for the body, she created another of the garden's delights . . . the butterfly.*

# Dixon

When Hugo and Margaret Dixon moved to Memphis, Tennessee, in 1940, they purchased a 17-acre tract of land studded with magnificent hardwood trees. Here they built their home and, with the help of Mr. Dixon's sister, noted landscape architect Hope Crutchfield, transformed the surrounding woodlands into shady gardens and walks reminiscent of the great English landscape parks. This style is developed on the premise that all of Nature is a garden, and the best designs appear always to have been there. Using this as a guide, they fashioned beautiful views and walks, skillfully emphasizing the old trees.

A sweeping vista encompassing several acres distinguishes the rear Dixon garden. From a site midway in the lawn, Grecian figures of the four seasons rise above white azaleas. From here, the cross-axis plan of the garden is clearly visible. With the house fixed at the northernmost point and the sculpture of Europa and the Bull at the south, the Terrace and statue of Venus of Memphis form the crosspiece. Each of these four points serves a specific purpose. A reflecting pool and an allée of azaleas frame the approach to the "Whispering Bench" area east of the house. A series of formal gardens is south of a reflecting pool and terraced down to meet a wide corridor with the Venus of Memphis marble sculpture, commissioned by the Dixons and completed in 1963 by Wheeler Williams, at the east terminus and a swimming pool, now covered for a terrace, anchoring the west terminus.

An Italian-style parterre garden is designed in three levels, each divided by an informal hedge of common boxwood. This small planting area incorporates a variety of colors, from the yellow of tulips to the pink and white of azaleas. The uppermost parterre is composed of geometric beds of yellow double Monte Carlo tulips. The center parterre contains the focal point of these gardens, the century-old bronze planter with cupids, one of a pair that once adorned a hallway in the eighteenth century Italian-style Mereworth Castle in Kent, England. Planted with Universal deep yellow, a new variety of pansy, this continues the yellow theme from the upper garden into the center. The lowest parterre consists of three concentric semicircles of pink and white azalea hedges.

One of the many other small groupings is the English Woodland Gardens. Here, paths and wooden bridges wander past colorful masses of American wildflowers, as well as columbine, phlox, poppy and foamflower. During the summer, this area is a woodland of textures and shades of green with ferns and hostas.

When the Dixons died in 1974, they generously left the gardens, along with their home and an endowment, in trust for the benefit of the public. The house has since been adapted as an art gallery, and today the Dixon Gallery and Gardens not only bring enjoyment to the public but serve as an educational facility for students of art and horticulture.

The Dixons' love of art and flowers carries into the rooms where floral arrangements complement paintings by artists who include Degas, Constable, Gainsborough, Boudin, Sisley, Monet, Chagall and Renoir.

LEFT: *In early spring, flowering trees and azaleas herald the beginning of a new season. Viewed from the porch of Dixon Gallery, an understory of white dogwoods glows beneath large oaks.*

ABOVE: *A stone statue representing one of the four seasons is set amid white azaleas and dogwoods.*

ABOVE: *Ferns, phlox, foamflowers and other perennials frame an informal bench in a tranquil woodland setting.*

FACING PAGE: *Pink, lily-flowered tulips and yellow pansies welcome visitors along a path in the gardens.*

FOLLOWING PAGES: *Throughout the year, container plantings accent the terrace at the edge of the south lawn.*

# Bellingrath

When Walter D. Bellingrath acquired a dilapidated fishing camp on the outskirts of Mobile, Alabama, 67 years ago, little did he envision its metamorphosis into the lovely retreat known as Bellingrath Gardens. Its transformation began when his wife Bessie planted a scattering of azaleas, the first infringement on "Mr. Bell's" previously all-male domain. One improvement led to another until the acreage was turned into a secluded estate that others would eventually clamor to see.

Since Mr. Bellingrath's wall of privacy came tumbling down more than 50 years ago, millions of people have visited the property, and its appeal remains strong. Though it may not be the matriarch of nationally known floral attractions, it is certainly the prima donna of year-round outdoor American gardens. Visitors are captivated by the charming grounds, which are situated on the picturesque banks of the Isle-aux-Oies River, and may also enjoy tours of the stately residence and an adjacent building where a magnificent Boehm porcelain collection is on display.

Once considered only a seasonal attraction offering a profuse display of azaleas and camellias, Bellingrath now prides itself on being a floral wonderland during every part of the year. Summer brings subtle changes in the Gulf Coast sunlight that plays upon the many pools and fountains, heightening the bright colors of the flowers, tropical foliage and overall greenery. Alamandas and roses, heavily accented by hydrangeas, periwinkle, daisies, salvia and fancy leaf foliage plants predominate during the summer months. As days shorten into fall, the gardens reach a striking pinnacle. During chrysanthemum season — late October and most of November — the world's largest display of mums adds the drama of massed color. Bedding plants along broad, tree-lined paths produce a panorama of color in late winter and early spring rivaling that of the azaleas.

With the advent of spring, many corners and niches of the vast semitropical acreage become bouquets of assorted flowers, including the first roses, all confirming the end of winter. Sections of the garden are blanketed by the color of approximately 140,000 tulips and other bulbs arranged with exquisite taste. More than 2,000 ornamental trees along pathways, in adjacent woods and in other border areas are in full bloom.

In September of 1979, Hurricane Frederick slashed through the area. It uprooted and topped most of the trees virtually destroying the idyllic setting. "While we shall always miss the venerable trees lost to the storm, the performance expected of the new ones will greatly enhance the garden's history," says George E. Downing, chairman of The Bellingrath-Morse Foundation. It was Mr. Downing's determination and resourcefulness that beat the odds in rebuilding the storm-torn attraction at a cost of more than $5 million.

The overall effect of the hurricane — the snake in this Eden — was to convert Bellingrath from a canopied retreat into a sunny one, with the collateral benefit of increased vitality and manicured formality generated by more sunshine. Four landscape engineers and scores of gardeners, aided by Mother Nature herself, keep this grande dame of American gardens in the manner to which she has long been accustomed.

LEFT: *Red and yellow tulips sparkle against a backdrop of evergreen shrubs, while a Japanese tulip magnolia offers a magnificent display of fragrant, purple flowers.*

ABOVE: *A rustic bridge crosses one end of Mirror Lake and the Rockery to an ever-changing panorama of bedding plants that complement shrubs and trees. In early spring, colorful tulips planted in a zig-zag pattern cover the hillside.*

191

FACING PAGE: *Spring is greeted with the festive foliage of daffodils and hyacinths around a terrace of the Bellingrath home. Pansies and snapdragons are planted in decorative containers.*

ABOVE: *A semicircular bed of tulips bordered with liriope enhances a portion of the Great Lawn.*

ABOVE: *A mass of chrysanthemums surrounding a teahouse is reflected in the Oriental-American Garden's tranquil lake.*

RIGHT: *In fall, beds of chrysanthemums ablaze with color are punctuated by unusual trees of red 'Fire Chief' and yellow 'Jane Hart' mums in a fanciful garden display.*

FACING PAGE: *Cascading chrysanthemums accent the flagstone wall and steps leading to the gardens.*

# Magnolia

The history of Magnolia Gardens, near Charleston, South Carolina, intertwines with the saga of Magnolia Plantation and the Drayton family members who have owned it for 300 years. Under their direction, these cherished gardens have become a scenic wonder renowned throughout the world.

The first Draytons came to the New World in the 17th century, when Thomas Drayton and his son left England to settle in Barbados. Thomas, Jr., moved to what was then called Charles Towne in the 1670's and acquired Magnolia Plantation through his marriage to Ann Fox. Here he built a mansion patterned after his ancestral home and planted a formal garden in the strict French style of the time of Louis XIV. This house burned in 1800, but was replaced by a three-story cypress structure built over a brick ground floor. In 1865, the house again met a fiery fate, this time at the hands of General Sherman's troops.

The original character of the gardens planted by Thomas Drayton, Jr., remained unchanged until The Reverend John Grimke Drayton took over his family's property. John Drayton's time came in the aftermath of the Civil War, and he was forced to sell 1,500 acres of the plantation's phosphate-rich land for a mere $25,000 in order to rebuild. To cut costs, he dismantled a pre-Revolutionary summer home he owned, barged it down-river to Magnolia and reconstructed it over the surviving brick first floor.

This third home, which is still owned by Drayton descendants, stands without any pretension to grandeur in its park-like setting, framed by green lawns, trees draped with Spanish moss and flowers blooming in every season. Today, the gardens themselves reflect the changes of John Drayton, who rebelled against traditional French design in favor of a less formal embellishment of the gardens' natural beauty.

In place of clipped hedges and geometric beds and walks, he introduced wandering paths and informal plantings. He took advantage of assets Nature provided by using the swamp cypress, indigenous to the area, as background for his azalea plantings. Today, propagations of these plants are mirrored in the dark waters of the surrounding lakes.

Financial necessity eventually persuaded the Draytons to open Magnolia Gardens for public admission. America's leading pictorial magazines of the time, *Picturesque America* and *Harper's*, featured it with extravagant comments, and its fame spread rapidly. In 1890, Baedecker's travel guide listed Magnolia Gardens, along with the Grand Canyon and Niagara Falls, as the foremost travel experiences in all of America.

During the last decade, there has been a second major horticultural revolution. For 300 years Magnolia Gardens existed largely as a spring display; but in recent years, through the introduction of thousands of flowering shrubs and bedding plants, Magnolia has become a showplace for all seasons. The main purpose of this change was to increase the year-round appeal and ensure its continued financial viability in the future.

Magnolia Gardens is a landmark and a tribute to the American spirit. It began in an untamed land, survived a devastating war, overcame financial setbacks and flourished despite all, growing more beautiful with each passing year.

PRECEDING PAGES: *Century-old live oaks draped with Spanish moss surround the approach to Magnolia Plantation House and Gardens near Charleston, South Carolina, the oldest major garden site in this hemisphere.*

FACING PAGE: *Images of flowers, trees and an intricately designed bridge are peacefully reflected in the dark lake.*

ABOVE: *A rustic bridge leads to woodland walks bordered by hundreds of Indica azalea varieties.*

FOLLOWING PAGE: *Ancient bald cypress trees awake with lacy green leaves in early spring.*

Garden Design

RESIDENCE

1 Sugar Maple
2 Washington Hawthorn
3 Single Trunk Pale Pink Crape Myrtle
4 Southern Magnolia

5 Boxwood
6 Pink or White Gumpo Azalea
7 Pink or White Indica Azalea
8 Topiary

9 Vinca Minor
10 Wisteria
11 Euonymus Kewensis
12 Mulch

13 Water Feature
14 Millstone
15 Bench
16 Brick Edging

# Winter

*N*ow that the season of "bare bones" landscapes has arrived, the way in which a basic design is seen — head-on or sideways — makes a difference, because the overall view will encompass every detail at once. Lawns, woodlands, gardens and driveways are all on display. Winter plans are greatly enriched by evergreens that are thoughtfully placed to act as screens, and this time of year is perfect for planting and relocating. All sizes of trees, shrubs and evergreen vines in an amazing number of varieties are available, so take time in choosing. Note which plants stand alone and which ones prefer close companions.

All sorts of progressive changes come into sharp focus during winter months. There is time to become acquainted with many new varieties of plant materials — not necessarily better, just new, and always interesting. Choices are not difficult when knowledge of the ultimate height of various plants is part of the workable plan; knowing what to expect results in a pruning program that works. Should the design call for a 16-foot plant, put *Viburnum sieboldi* in the appropriate spot. If there is a longing for mass screening about 6 feet high in a somewhat different material, loropetalum will accommodate this need and will require only light pruning once a year just after the shredded coconut-like flowers have stopped blooming.

When seen head-on during winter, trees against the sky above the roof of a house form a backdrop for everything in front of them. A house whose roofline makes a slash across an empty sky needs great assistance to be anchored to its surroundings. Oaks, hickories and maples cannot be expected to grow quickly — they hurry for no one. Instead, consider the following, none of which waste any growing time: Virginia pines, tulip poplars (*Liriodendron*), weeping and swamp willows, tupelos, also known as black gum (*Nyssa*), Southern sugar maples (*Acer floridanum*), goldenrain trees (*Koelreuteria*) and Japanese pagoda trees (*Sophora*). For future beauty, plant other favored varieties in front of that initial work force and watch the development of a stunning setting.

Of all the design problems which seem to become acute during December, January and February, one of the most troublesome is that of the entrance of a house seen from the side. Often the doorway is not evident from the walkway leading to it; instead, a view of the neighbor's lot is all too sharp a focal point. So begin planning handsome evergreen screening of *Viburnum macrophyllum*, Nellie Stevens holly or Fortune osmanthus. If location makes it possible, also consider planting one variety of *Camellia japonica*. In front of any of these, place a well-proportioned bench with back and arms. In such a setting, the front door area comes into view easily, especially if the material surrounding this most important of areas is reduced in size by judicious pruning or replaced with dwarf plant material.

Winter is the perfect time to decide on the direction and shape of woodland paths. Since there is no towering bloom or berry-bearing growth just now, distractions are at a minimum, so stake out center lines for paths. It is easy to retrace steps, change markers and turn in another direction until the walk is pleasing. Edge it, if possible, with small logs or split lengths of oak, cedar or cypress and cover the floor of the path with pine straw. Wildflowers and groups of ferns can now be set along the edge of paths.

### Hints for Winter

**December:** This is the best time to plant bare-rooted trees and is the last call for tulip planting. Continue planting roses and all kinds of shrubs where needed. If necessary to transplant boxwood, do it this month. Do no digging if the soil is frozen. Among some interesting winter trees is the American hornbeam, characteristically open and spreading at the crown. It has contorted and folded bark that is extremely muscular-looking. One of the prettiest little lawn trees, full of long fern-like compound leaves and long bunches of yellow flowers in the growing season, is the goldenrain tree. In winter, when the leaves are gone, its brown fruits and variegated dark and red bark are pleasing to the eye.

**January:** Seeds of cornflowers, sweet peas and larkspur will still be successful if planted during good weather or when the snow has melted. Never cover peonies; they love to freeze. New shrubs can be safely planted if the ground has thawed. Shrubs in bloom include daphne, January jasmine, tea olive, winter sweet, witch hazel and Christmas honeysuckle.

**February:** New perennials can be planted now; established plants can be divided and replanted. Plant broadleaf evergreens and cut out dead wood from flowering trees; prune fruit trees.

RESIDENCE

1 Flowering Hawthorn or Kousa Dogwood    3 Pink or White Azalea    5 Spring Blooming Perennials
2 Mammouth Crocus Blooming in Vinca    4 Purple or White Wisteria

# Spring

Probably the most bewitching season of the year is spring, when Nature takes over with its masses of color to create unbelievable glory. It is a time when enthusiastic gardeners are inspired to plant flower varieties long admired but never tried.

During this rejuvenation period, when spring's amazing softening process tends to absorb some of man's misguided choices, is the time to take a second look at unbalanced benches, weak topiaries and statues of doubtful merit. On the other hand, springtime quickly accepts a well-placed, carefully selected point of interest. When choosing locations, go slowly instead of attempting to solve all problems in one day.

Walls and fences in muted tones make good backdrops for topiaries, which are our prima donnas and must have center stage. Stone and marble statues are stunning with backgrounds of beautiful dark green shrubs such as upright yew, podocarpus, boxwood, Hinoki cypress and hemlock. And a little water works wonders; a jet sparkling in the sunlight as it rises from a small pool draws the eye as no other feature can. Evergreen background planting, higher than the jet, steadies the composition. In such situations, boxwood and Fortune osmanthus are well known for their fine holding quality. Foregrounds of springtime ground cover — crocuses, jonquils, narcissus, early tulips and daffodils emerging from carpets of periwinkle — will make fond memories.

Planning ahead eliminates calamities and allocates a vital role for each segment of the design. Take paths and walkways, for instance: they can carve otherwise attractive compositions into narrow pointed areas resembling pieces of pie. Walkways should lead the eye toward special focal points, but unfortunately, may direct attention to groups of meaningless shrubs. Worse still, some lead to open spots where absolutely nothing exists. Imagine paths as lines of stitching, sewing all pieces easily and harmoniously into one complete work, and plants will breathe again.

Spring gardens bulge with many colors, and a little research enables the gardener to plan for prolonged beauty. Check on blooming dates so that one flowering plant family can blend into the next, allowing colors to flow into summer without pause. Snowdrops may be a garden's first occupant, then crocus, alyssum, hyacinth, wallflower, pansy and narcissus. Such early beauties will overlap columbine, thrift, primrose, scilla, dwarf iris and Virginia bluebell. Chinese magnolias followed by dogwoods are always special, particularly when accompanied by baby's breath, spirea, deciduous azaleas, white and pale pink quince and Scotch broom. Savor the great beauty of all varieties of evergreen azaleas, beginning with the Kurume family and ending with late Macrantha and Gumpo. Be sure to take notes during each season so all will be easier the next time around.

Many people claim that spring flowers and foliage should be let alone to grow rampant over entire hillsides. Actually there is nothing more beautiful, especially if one is not involved in upkeep. It is a fact, however, that honeysuckle, poison ivy, wild Elaeagnus, sedge grass and day lilies spread more quickly and grow higher than more desirable plants and will overtake that favorite hillside. Casual care will not make a difference, either; there must be regular, militant attacks.

## Hints for Spring

**March:** List favorite daffodil varieties while they are in bloom and plan to order more for fall. Do not disturb areas where seeds of pale pink celosia were broadcast last fall; they will be showing soon. When cleaning up winter's twigs and leaves, rake lightly or hand-pick to protect tiny plants; there could be larkspur, cornflowers, Shirley poppies and snow-on-the-mountain. Feed pansies that have bloomed in good weather all winter.

**April:** Have soil analyzed if this has not been done for some time. Add the appropriate well-balanced fertilizer and topsoil. Plant seeds the last week in April. They will come up fast, so watch for overcrowding; transplant seedlings and mulch. Divide perennials, and plant new roses. Add new varieties of hosta; they will be there forever. Plant summer flowering bulbs such as cannas, Peruvian daffodils, tuberoses and specially colored gladioli. Add native silver bell (*Halesia*) and fringe trees (*Chionanthus*) to wooded areas.

**May:** Plant seeds of solid-color giant zinnias, lemon yellow marigolds and yellow and pink celosia to provide plenty of cut flowers all summer and fall. Watch for weeds. Thin celosia seedlings so they will not overtake the garden. Plant impatiens in hanging baskets and in every semishady nook and cranny. Check thin grass spots; add seeds of hulled bermuda or sprigs of hybrid bermuda and Meyer or Matrella zoysia. Trees can be planted now; if special care is taken when staking, watering and fertilizing.

RESIDENCE

1  Blooming Gumpo Azalea under     2  Flowering Crape Myrtle     4  Summer Annuals
   Hawthorn or/Kousa Dogwood       3  Flowering Magnolia

# Summer

As spring flowers begin to fade, it's time to concentrate on the summer garden spectacles. Breathing space is vital to plants in midsummer. Flowers, shrubs and vines all become drooping and listless when packed in tight masses. But when sufficient breathing room is provided, plants develop better and are far easier to maintain.

Though a high evergreen hedge completely surrounding an outdoor garden ensures privacy, it will constrict air flow and may seem too confining. Consider interspersing lattice panels or pierced brick walls within the hedge to allow summer breezes to pass through the garden.

White phlox, lemon-yellow daylilies, perennial forget-me-nots and pale pink impatiens add charm to any summer garden. Green and white is a delightful combination, but be careful to feature only a few of the best examples against dark green backgrounds. Plant only three or four green-and-white English hollies against a group of deep green hemlocks, or place twelve green-and-white caladiums in front of solid green aucuba.

Do your best to stay ahead of rampant summer growth. For instance, don't allow seedling mimosas to develop unchecked; they are pushy and will sprout everywhere. So will Elaeagnus, which seems to grow overnight through the middle of choice azaleas, boxwoods, hydrangeas or any nearby plant. Seedling cherry laurels and wild cherries will literally bend gentler trees over if let alone; wild cherries always provide a home for bagworms. All of this is a nuisance, so be alert and take regular inspection tours.

The scents of summer! Remember that first delicious smell of a nasturtium border in hot sun? Or nicotiana in the evening? Flower perfume is enchanting because it hangs upon the summer air. Lay out a path alongside fragrant tea olives or cover a terrace arbor with moonvines. What an experience it is to watch the vines' lovely, fragrant white flowers open during a summer night and cover every available space with simple, uncomplicated beauty! Buddleia (butterfly bush), vitex and Persian lilac bear flowers of similar shape, and all produce delightful perfume.

And roses: everyone has a favorite, but Tropicana's fragrance is hard to better. Herb gardens have been with us since the Pilgrims arrived, and nothing is more appealing or aromatic in hot sun. Surround such special areas with boxwood hedges, anise trained on walls, pink honeysuckle on fences or sweet peas on trellises.

While summer plants are developing, cover those in-between spaces with seeds of portulaca, which bloom in many colors in hot sun all summer. You can easily carry out the same idea by planting dwarf impatiens in shade. But let us not leave blank areas to their own devices; is there anything more oppressive-looking than a patch of weeds? Meet force with force and crowd them out.

A section where woodlands meet grass may be neatly stopped by many kinds of ferns in groups. Should the collapsed appearance of ferns in winter be a worry, plant late blooming Gumpo azaleas between clusters of ferns.

Simplifying designs and choosing flowers in pale color tones make your surroundings appear cooler in summer.

### Hints for Summer

**June:** Mulch shrubs, roses and vegetable beds with pine straw to help them withstand the heat. Water late in the day; the more mulch, the less water needed. Potted plants are in danger if they are forgotten for one day. Plant tuberoses, but only a few because of their heavy perfume. Add tubers of small dahlias and corms of pale green and pure white gladioli. Impatiens seeds planted now will present a delightful dividend in the fall. Favorite annuals can still be planted.

**July:** In watering, soak the ground thoroughly. When beautiful copper or pale pink celosias go to seed, shake the seeds over beds when you clear them out. Sow carrot and lettuce seeds for fall harvesting. Cut old flowers off crape myrtles to encourage a second bloom. If a tree form is the right shape for its location, do not cut off trunks or branches; this is unnecessary and can be quite destructive. Add new zinnia and marigold plants wherever needed. Don't feed roses, but stay on a regular spray schedule. Hold back all chrysanthemums and dahlias by pinching off buds.

**August:** Weeds come with the territory but are easier to eliminate when mulch is plentiful. Pinch back snapdragons for a second bloom and try to keep dead flowers off all plants. Disbud camellias; this chore will produce fine results. Sow pansy seeds if you are patient. Any variety of begonia will benefit from top dressings of dried cow manure. To produce fine chrysanthemum and dahlia blooms, use liquid manure every two weeks until buds appear. Plant fescue and rye grass if the weather at the end of the month is cool.

RESIDENCE

1 Chrysanthemums replace summer annuals    2 Mulch    3 Brilliant fall color of Sugar Maple, Hawthorn, Kousa Dogwood and Crape Myrtle

In fall, flowers, trees and shrubs seem to have a sense of urgency, to want to squeeze out every drop of color before winter starts rattling the door. There is nothing in any season to match the beauty of a sunny fall afternoon; then, plants concentrate on producing the very finest red, yellow, orange, pink or purple. They are not about to spend this beauty in summer's heat but wait patiently for their time to come.

September is neither summer nor winter, and it's a month when the gardener wonders what to do, if anything. Relax . . . there is actually no need for any great hustle, except to check watering and mulching. But some planting can be done. For instance, install a compact new flower border consisting of cushion and tall chrysanthemums in clear yellows, whites and pinks. Add plumes of copper, pale pink and yellow celosias and border the bed with dwarf ageratum.

Several suggestions: it is easier to work with slightly raised beds than with those flat on the ground; you can work flower beds not over four feet from front to back without falling into them or walking among the plants; provide the bed a background without roots, such as low fencing, a lattice, the wall of the house or a freestanding brick or stone wall.

October is a fine month to try out various shapes and sizes of garden ornaments. Fountains, boxes, urns, pots, figures of rabbits or turtles and the like will now be seen as perfectly charming or as definite disasters without the aesthetic support of deciduous plants. View them from every angle for a few days and decide which enhance your design.

Often creeping bareness spreads as winter approaches. When such specimen plants as fully developed Foster, Savannah or Nellie Stevens hollies are located in vital spots, they warm the surroundings immediately and glisten in the autumn sun. Plant material native to your area of the South is a great boon toward easier maintenance.

The hardy broadleaf and needle-like evergreens are plants that remain handsome regardless of time of year. There are others that are obviously uncomfortable in the fall and do not enrich the plan. Crape myrtle and river birch are stunning anytime, but weeping willows are not, so care must be taken in their placement. Only after autumn has passed do we realize how helpful it is to see all plants in action or inaction. Spacing produces beauty or dreariness, so take time to measure. A magnolia screen, for instance, should have its trunks 10 feet on center so the branches of each tree may overlap the other. The use to which plants are put governs their spacing.

Water knows no season and is as exciting in November as it is in April; in fall, consider piping it over a small stone spillway. Gouge out an area on a small slope and situate large rocks artistically in this hollowed-out site. Surround it with pine straw framed with groups of colchicums (autumn-blooming crocuses), then plant native evergreen leucothoe on each side of the running water. This beautiful plant will trail its long fingers over the ground and soften the appearance of the stones. In this composition, or used as background material, *Ilex latifolia* is a distinct addition.

### Hints for Fall

**September:** Anticipate spring by ordering daffodils, tulips, scillas and crinums, but do not plant them this month. Study other gardeners' successful fall flower beds and follow their lead. Learn how to transplant seedlings, divide daylilies and irises and sow pansy and stock seeds. Plant ryegrass now if needed. Reserve space in vegetable beds or cut-flower beds for seeds of lettuce and onions and plant them before this month is over. Divide perennials if necessary and group them to become the backbone of the flower border.

**October:** Dig up caladiums and save the best. Shifting and adding shrubs and trees is pleasant work now, especially when the gardener has a workable plan. Plant daffodils, tulips and pansies before the soil becomes hard from the cold. Add native plants to garden and woodland this year. Fothergillas, serviceberry (*Amelanchier*), wild azaleas, oak leaf hydrangeas and leucothoe are hardy and handsome. Native tupelo (*Nyssa*) and sourwood (*Oxydendrum arboreum*) produce spectacular color all of October. Now is the time to plant sweet peas, larkspur and cornflowers.

**November:** Cut back perennial phlox and hardy asters 2 to 3 inches above ground. Newly planted roses will welcome mounds of soil and mulch placed around them. Continue to plant shrubs, vines and trees as needed. Now is the time to take on the thankless job of checking drainage in the entire garden area. Add tulip and daffodil bulbs where needed. Plant extra bulbs of all colors in rows in the vegetable garden for cutting. Make brief notes on what is planted and the location. The great house plant moving — from outside to inside — should be finished by now.

# Credits

VILLA CARO
photography by Jonathan Hillyer

A COUNTRY COTTAGE
photography by David I. Durham III
and Tom Woodham

BRIGADOON
photography by R. Cotten Alston

FRENCH FLAVOR
photography by Paul G. Beswick

TOPIARY MAGIC
photography by Derek Fell

ROMANTIC CLOISTER
photography by Paul G. Beswick

THE WHITE HOUSE
photography by Taylor Lewis

FORMAL CITYSCAPE
photography by Deloye R. Burrell

BANKSHAVEN
photography by Paul G. Beswick
and Sutlive/Warren

MILBURNE
photography by Paul G. Beswick

A TOUCH OF NORMANDY
photography by Deloye R. Burrell

RENAISSANCE VISION
photography by Derek Fell

PLANNED PERFECTION
photography by Max Eckert

BILTMORE
photography by James Valentine and
Cheryl Sales (Courtesy Biltmore Estate)

MIDDLETON
photography by Derek Fell

ORTON
photography by James Valentine

ELIZABETHAN
photography by Paul G. Beswick

WINTERTHUR
photography by Derek Fell

LONGUE VUE
photography by John Rogers, Irwin McAdams, and
Frank Gordon and Son

TRYON PALACE
photography by Paul G. Beswick (Courtesy Tryon
Palace Gardens)

CYPRESS
photography by Derek Fell

BAYOU BEND
photography by Rob Muir (Courtesy Bayou Bend
Gardens Endowment), Ogden Robertson and
Blaine Hickey

DIXON
photography by Steve Hogben

BELLINGRATH
photography by Deloye R. Burrell

MAGNOLIA
photography by Ogden Robertson and Blaine Hickey

The following writers prepared the original
SOUTHERN ACCENTS' articles from which the
material in this book has been adapted:

Howard Barney, Ann W. Barrett, Leslie E. Benham,
Mary Wallace Crocker, Timothy Dunford, Derek Fell,
Edith Henderson, Susan L. Hewitt, Betsy Kent,
George C. Longest, Anita Morrison Mobley, Janet S.
Moore, Bonnie Warren, Susannah M. Wilson and
Tom Woodham.

Original text and captions adapted by Helen C. Griffith.

Book design and production by Corinne Cox, Atlanta.

Garden design consultant, Edith Henderson,
Landscape Architect, FASLA, Atlanta.
Garden illustrations by Thea Lloyd.

Color Separations by Atlanta Color Concepts, Inc.,
and Graphics International, Atlanta.

Printed and bound in Italy by Arnoldo Mondadori,
Editore, Verona.

# Acknowledgements

SOUTHERN ACCENTS Press
Senior Editors: Helen C. Griffith and Sallie S. Stevens
Associate Editor: Shelby M. Neely
Copy Editor: Ann W. Barrett
Production Assistants: Joan Sennette, Margaret Savage, Susan Wozny
Typography: Barbara K. Allen, Debby H. Daniel and Robert M. Adams
Fulfillment Services Manager: Shielia Pearce
Promotion Manager: Connie Nesbit
Director of Public Relations: Elsie Moses
Project Consultant: Raymond E. Hebert

SOUTHERN ACCENTS Press is a division of W.R.C. Smith Publishing Company, Atlanta, Georgia
President: Walter M. Mitchell, Jr.
Vice President: Sims Bray, Jr.
Vice President/Finance: Sara H. Smith
Secretary/Treasurer: Shirley C. Howell

SOUTHERN ACCENTS Magazine
Editor-In-Chief: Lisa B. Newsom
Associate Editor: Helen C. Griffith
Managing Editor: Diane D. Burrell
Senior Editors: Susan L. Hewitt, Susannah M. Wilson, and Leslie E. Benham
Copy Editor: Ann W. Barrett
Special Projects Editor: Sallie S. Stevens
Design Editor: Harvey Bourland
Circulation Director: Shielia Pearce
Circulation Manager: Nancy Clark
Customer Services Manager: Abigail Pettiss
Advertising Manager: Marilynn LaHatte
Art Director: Oscar Almeida
Production Director: Connie Nesbit
Production Manager: Patricia Seale
Mechanical Graphics: Joan Sennette
Typography: Barbara K. Allen and Robert M. Adams

We would like to thank the homeowners who graciously consented to include their gardens in this book: Mr. William N. Banks, Mr. and Mrs. Tench C. Coxe III, Mr. and Mrs. Homer L. Deakins, Jr., Mr. and Mrs. De Jongh Franklin, Mr. Ryan Gainey, Mr. and Mrs. Jim Gibbs, Mrs. D. Luke Hopkins, Mr. and Mrs. D.E. Hughes, Mr. and Mrs. Thomas E. Martin, Jr., Mr. and Mrs. Michael McDowell, Mrs. Walter Robertson, and Mrs. Henry Tompkins.